The
CONFIDENT
Child

The
CONFIDENT
Child

12 STEPS TO BOOST YOUR CHILD'S
CONFIDENCE AND SELF-ESTEEM

JESSICA PALMER

TABLE OF CONTENTS

YOUR FREE GIFT

As a way of saying thanks for your purchase, I'm offering a few free bonuses exclusive to readers of *The Positive Child* and *The Confident Child*.

Within the bonuses, you'll discover a collection of printable mindfulness checklists, a helpful video, and a bonus monthly calendar. Access the link below to get free instant access.

http://bit.ly/palmerbonus

INTRODUCTION

No parents like to see their children struggle. It is not easy to see your child feel sad, lonely or depressed. Usually, parents try to cheer their kids up by giving them all sorts of materialistic things. It might momentarily cheer the child up, but it is not a permanent solution. If only throwing money at a problem could make it disappear! By buying them joy, you are wrongly conditioning their young minds to believe they are entitled to whatever they want, merely because they are upset.

If you want your child to be happier, score better grades at school, be a better person and be a generally happy and content individual, then self-confidence is the solution. Self-confidence is the belief in one's own self and abilities. Armed with self-confidence, your child will lead a happier and fuller life.

Why am I so sure that self-confidence is the key to a child's overall wellbeing? It's because I have learned this lesson through experience. Hello, I am Jessica Palmer, and I am a proud mother of four delightful children. 22 years of motherhood has taught me plenty about children, their psychology, and their needs. Two of my kids are in college, and the other two are close to completing their high school education. I have and still am doing everything I possibly can to make them confident and as mentally sharp as they probably can be.

During this journey, I had a lot to learn. I made a couple of mistakes, and I learned my lessons too. My experience prompted me to write a book containing the secrets to a child's happiness. I want to share my knowledge with all parents who require a little help in parenting their little ones. In this book, I will share with you all the things that I did right, which helped strengthen the bond I share with my kids and also strengthen our family as a whole.

All parents wish that their children should get all the happiness they deserve. The first step toward attaining it is developing confidence. By improving their confidence now, you can ensure that they become successful and happy with their accomplishments. This is because they have the internal strength required not just to identify what they want, but also to pursue their hopes and dreams fearlessly and boldly. The various tips and strategies I have provided in this book helped my children become confident during their childhood. They are all blossoming into wonderful adults who don't hesitate to chase their goals.

Obtaining and living a happier life for children as well as families is a topic that I am quite familiar with. As a parent, I fully understand our responsibilities towards our children. We must provide them with the confidence they require to lead a full and happy life. Whenever I have shared my insights and tips with others, I received positive feedback. Initially, I used to share my ideas with just my family members and friends. After a while, I realized that the information I possess could be quite valuable to other parents too. The various tips and steps discussed in this book will bring families closer, help children become happier individuals, and also improve a parent's confidence in their ability to parent.

Dealing with four kids has taught me plenty. I will guide you along the way as you help your child become more confident and happier. I promise that by the end of this book, you will have gained a lot of invaluable insight about your child's development and psyche.

I believe that the best gift a parent can give their

children is a healthy sense of self-confidence. You can certainly buy your children whatever they desire, but there is so much more to life than mere worldly possessions. Wouldn't it be better to teach your child to lead a happier life than buying them a toy?

Well, the good news is that self-confidence can be easily taught. The various tips and tricks provided in this book, along with the different strategies, are quite useful. The information given in this book is divided into simple chapters, and each of these chapters provide various practical steps you can use. If you start following the tips given in this book, your child will become a better person. If you want to see your kids accomplish their goals in life and attain the success they desire, then this is the perfect book for you!

Most parents are so focused on their kid's short-term happiness that they forget about long-term happiness. Concentrating on the kid's short-term satisfaction will make them feel better, but only momentarily. However, what will happen once this moment passes by? The challenges and obstacles will not go away. A lot of parents are so protective of their kids that they let them live in a bubble. The real world certainly doesn't function this way, and the minute they step into the real world, this bubble bursts. All such children are then left to deal with crippling anxiety, lack of self-confidence, low self-esteem, and self-doubt. No one can deal with all these things all of a sudden and all at once. It takes practice and effort. Therefore, the sooner you teach your kids to be confident, the more successful they will be in life.

Another mistake I have seen a lot of parents make is this: They believe that they are truly responsible for their kid's happiness. If you start assuming responsibility for all that your child feels, then it is quite likely that you will never fully allow your child to deal with his or her emotions. As tempted as you might be to swoop in, and fight your child's worries away, stop yourself from doing this. Your child must learn to deal with their emotions and learn to take control of their life.

So, without further ado, let us read on and learn.

CHAPTER 1

Improve Your Own Confidence

There are a couple of things you must teach yourself before learning about ways to improve your child's self-esteem and confidence. The first set of behavior a child learns is usually from his parents or guardians. If you want your child to become confident, then you must portray and project confidence. As their parents, you must embody confidence. It is important that you work on yourself before trying to help your child.

Trying to be a perfectionist seldom guarantees perfection. Most of us, in our bid to attain the elusive perfection, often set ourselves up for disappointment. In my 22 years of motherhood, if there is one fact that I have come to accept truly, it is this: The concept of being a perfect parent doesn't exist. All that you can do is try to be your best self and perform to the best of your abilities. You cannot do more than this, and if you think you can be a perfect parent, you are merely setting yourself up for disappointment. You are human, too, and it is only natural to make a couple of mistakes along the way. At times, your emotions get the better of you, or there might be times when you might not know how to cope with stressful situations.

Different factors influence the way you manage stressful situations. Factors such as your upbringing to the life experiences you've had and other situational factors all play an essential role in your ability to handle stress. Just like any other human being, even parents express emotions and at times, might slip up and give in to their unreasonable demands. If this is happening to you, then let me reassure you that it is normal. Every parent goes through this; you don't have to feel ashamed. The only thing that honestly matters to your child is that you are doing a good job. I'm not suggesting that it is okay to be a neglectful parent. It is never all right to ignore your child's well-being, but it is not okay when you don't do a good enough job all the time. Even if you make any parenting mistakes, keep in mind that you are human and can always fix your errors and work to ensure you don't repeat the same in the future. It will give you a good idea about the things you must and mustn't do while parenting your child. Well, at least this is what I have learned in my years as a parent.

Even if you make a mistake, it is important that you do not allow the guilt associated with it get the better of you and continue moving forward instead. If you doubt yourself or have low self-esteem, it will certainly have a negative influence on the relationship you share with your child. It might even affect their self-esteem. I'm sure you may have had moments where you wonder if you have been a good enough parent to your little one or if you're doing a good job. You'll learn about the different ways in which you can learn to manage emotions, improve your self-esteem, and in turn, help improve the quality of the relationship you share with your child. Apart from this, you will also understand your perspective about parenting and the way you view yourself as a parent.

I believe that all humans are born with an inherent need to connect with others. So, it is not surprising that the need to establish and form secure and nourishing relationships is something we crave and desire. We tend to have this undeniable desire to create a safe and nourishing relationship with our children. The self-esteem and confidence projected by a child who has a healthy and secure attachment with his parents will be greater than a child who doesn't have all this. There are three simple truths you must accept, and they are as follows.

- You will make mistakes while parenting, everyone does, and you don't have to worry.
- You must try your best and put in your 100%.
- You must let go of any illusions you have. Perfection doesn't exist, and the more you continue keeping that as your benchmark, the more disappointed you will be.

You can be the best parent you possibly can for your child, but that's about it, you can't call that perfect parenting. The simple tips given will enable you to be the kind of parent your child needs.

What is your general opinion about your parenting skills? If you aren't too happy with yourself as a parent, then it is quite likely that you might also be unsatisfied with different aspects of your life, personal or professional. The best way to discover the answer to these questions is via self-reflection. If you aren't sure where to start, then here are a few simple questions you can use to get started with self-reflection.

- What is your self-perception of your role as a parent?
- If you could make any changes, what would you change?
- What are the areas where you think you excel as a parent?
- How do you describe your parent-child relationship?
- If your child had to describe your characteristics, how would he do this?

Take some time, sit down by yourself, carefully think about your answers to these questions and make a note of them.

About Self-Esteem

Before you learn about ways you can improve your self-esteem and confidence as a parent, it is vital to determine what you think about yourself. Low self-esteem will have a negative effect on all aspects of your life, and parenting is not an exception. As a parent, you will need to make certain decisions for the wellbeing of your child. A lot of these decisions will not be easy. If you keep second-guessing yourself, you will barely make any progress with your child. Also, if you don't have the confidence required to stand by your decisions and enforce them, you cannot expect your child to listen to you. Rather, you would set a poor example for your child.

There are different reasons that can cause low self-esteem. The most common causes include having a depreciated sense of self-image and constantly thinking negative thoughts about yourself. The underlying causes include being subjected to neglect or abuse as a child, dealing with extremely critical and judgmental parents, and not getting adequate care and love from your parents. The other factors include dealing with extremely protective parents while growing up and dealing with stressful life experiences early on in life. Any negative life experiences you had to deal with, either at home or school will have a profound impact on your self-esteem. Harboring any negative core beliefs about yourself or your abilities can also dampen your self-confidence.

I am sure you must be wondering what these negative core beliefs are. A core belief is a deep-seated idea you have about yourself. We all tend to have a continuous internal dialogue going on in our heads. This internal self-talk is not undesirable, but when most of your core beliefs take a negative hue, it becomes undesirable. All the 'I' statements you make about yourself on a subconscious level are your core beliefs. For instance, you might have certain negative core beliefs like "I don't belong here," "I am not worthy of being loved," "I am worthless," "I am not good enough," "I am flawed," "I am not lovable," so on and so forth. If any of these core beliefs sound somewhat familiar to you, then it is time for a little self reflection. The one thing that's common among all the core beliefs is the feeling of not being good enough. Make a list of your negative core beliefs and think about the things, situations, people, or life experiences that have made you come to such conclusions.

I've mentioned that low self-esteem will harm your parenting practices; it might lead to negative parenting, or you might not even have the confidence about the way you parent. Apart from this, it might also make you feel bad about your parenting style. Negative parenting includes low acceptance of your child and low parental approval. Factors like this can cause severe harm to a parent-child relationship. Apart from this, it can also harm your child's budding self-esteem and self-confidence.

Before you learn about the ideal way to parent your child, you must learn about certain unhelpful styles of parenting. The three unhelpful styles are mean (authoritarian), weak (laissez-faire), and gone (neglectful or absent). A mean style of parenting is wherein a parent firmly believes that a child deserves to be punished whenever he is disobedient. Different forms of punishment include yelling, physical punishment, threats, and anything that will scare the child into obeying his parents. Usually, in this style of parenting, the parent tends to have a rather severe emotional reaction to their child's behavior. This kind of parenting only weakens the parent-child bond and doesn't do either of you any good.

If the mean style of parenting lies on one end of the spectrum, then weak parenting lies on the other end. This is as terrible as the previous one. Every child must feel secure and safe. For this, there needs to be a routine, structure, and specific boundaries. When these things are absent, the child will not feel secure. It can be rather scary and overwhelming when the child realizes that there is no one in charge. Let us assume that a child struggles with anger issues, and the parent does nothing to help the child manage his emotions. The child will have to learn by himself how to deal with his emotions.

This brings me to the final type of undesirable parenting. In this style of parenting, the parents are usually absent from their child's life. I am not talking about those instances when you can't take care of your child due to some health troubles or any office-related short trips. These are fine. Instead, I am talking about those parents who are almost always absent from their child's life. It essentially applies to all those parents who are dependent on and abuse drugs or alcohol. Parents who never give preference to their child's needs fall into this category. A parent is emotionally and at times, even physically absent from their child's life.

- So, what do you feel about your style of parenting?
- What do you think kids need from their parents?

Start maintaining a parenting journal wherein you make a note of your ideas, thoughts, opinions, and beliefs as a parent. You might be able to readily answer these questions, but spend some time on self-reflection, you will get more ideas. Make a note of these ideas and thoughts in the journal.

A child needs his or her parents to be kind, wise, and strong. If you struggle with low self-esteem, then this might not be an easy goal to accomplish. To learn about all this, read on.

Steps to Follow

Let go of the illusion of perfection; your child doesn't desire perfection. Having a good enough parent will suffice. There is nothing wrong with being a good enough parent. A good parent knows that all those negative core beliefs aren't entirely right, and instead of strengthening them, he will try and analyze them using honesty while withholding his judgment. If you do this, you will understand where you are doing well and the areas where you lag. Here are some steps you must follow to improve your self-esteem as a parent.

Accept

The way you parent your child is predominantly influenced by the way you were parented. There might have been instances where you caught yourself saying and behaving the way your parents used to in the past. These might be instances where you promised yourself that you wouldn't behave like your parents. However, when push comes to shove, do you see yourself imitating the same old patterns? Most of this is associated with the simple concept that most of the things you know about parenting come from your personal experience. You learn about parenting a child through different interactions you have with him every single day. Do you ever catch yourself thinking that you wouldn't want to pass on a specific trait or behavior to your little one? If yes, then you aren't alone. All those individuals who enter parenthood usually know about things that they don't like about their childhood and how they would want to parent their kids. It is not always easy to translate these thoughts and actions. To be a good parent, you must first understand and reflect upon your upbringing and then make choices about your style of parenting.

As a parent, it is your obligation to help your child develop not just physically, but emotionally as well as mentally. If you want to support his emotional development, then you must pay attention to the way you process your emotions. It is time for a little introspection. Dig deep and honestly examine the way you manage and deal with your emotions.

Think about all the primary emotions and the way your parents supported you to manage each of these emotions. You can also perform this exercise by analyzing the way different caregivers in your life helped you and your emotional development. For instance, whenever you felt sad, how did your parents respond to it? Did they get upset or did they try to make you feel better? Or did they give you your space to make sense of your emotions and identify what you're feeling? The way your parents dealt with your emotions will influence the way you deal with your child's emotions. While doing this exercise, remember that you're not trying to change your parents but are trying to understand how your own personal experiences have shaped you as an individual.

There are three important lessons you learned from this exercise. The first lesson is that we all learn about parenting from our parents or primary caregivers. The second lesson is that the ability to opt for a different style of parenting lies in your hands. The third lesson stresses the importance of self-reflection. When you reflect upon your childhood, it will help you determine whether you must do something or not.

Understand

Now that you've taken stock of the emotional support you received during your childhood, it is time to work on your triggers. Start making a note of the following points in the parenting journal.

- Are there any emotions that your child needs help to deal with, but you are unable to help him?
- How do you respond whenever your child expresses a big emotion?

- Do you think your response is positive or undesirable?

If you feel uneasy whenever your child expresses a specific emotion, then such an emotion expressed by a child is your trigger. It is usually a sign that you're getting a little too close to a specific memory of yours. Maybe you were taught that a specific emotion was not safe. All this is normal; all people struggle with a couple of emotions. However, if you want to be of any help to your child, then you must understand these emotions. Whenever you feel like this uneasiness is creeping up on you, pause and step back. Don't react the way you usually do, instead, give yourself a break. This will help calm you down and enable you to process the situation rationally.

The three simple steps for this exercise are as follows. The first one is that you must spend some time and think about all those emotions that a child displays, which makes you uneasy. Now, think about ways in which you can respond to those emotions or the way you usually respond to those emotions. The final step is to think about how you would want to respond to situations in the future.

Support

The relationship you share with your child must rest on a strong foundation if you want a secure attachment. This helps fuel your child's self-esteem and teaches him how to regulate his emotions in a relationship. Whenever your child experiences a difficult emotion, you must stay with him. This simple act will give him the emotional support required to deal with it. Apart from this, it also teaches him about empathy. Take a moment and think about it. How would you feel if instead of helping you handle your emotions, someone tries to talk you out of it? I am sure you wouldn't like this, well neither does your child. So, you must learn to support him regardless of what you feel at that moment. Your child needs you, and he will depend on you.

The three points you must keep in mind as follows. Children don't understand empathy, it is a skill you must teach them. If you want your child to be empathic, then you must display empathy. To build a secure and healthy parent-child relationship, then you must spend more time with your child. Spending time with your child means being present physically, emotionally, as well as mentally. And finally, if you feel like you are struggling with your emotions, then seek professional help.

Be Better

Try to be kinder, wiser, and stronger for your child. You must not only establish that you are in charge, but must do this in a manner that's infused with warmth, kindness, and care. For instance, if you notice that your child is throwing a tantrum about not getting to eat another slice of cake before dinner, what would you do? Instead of getting upset or punishing the child, try a different approach. Maybe you can say something along the lines of, "I know you aren't too happy that you cannot eat more cake before dinner. But it will be dinner time in ten minutes, and I don't want you to fill your tummy up right now." By doing this, you have not only acknowledged your child's disappointment and shown empathy but have also set a clear boundary and explained your reasons for doing the same.

The three takeaways from this aren't that you must be a better version of yourself. You must learn to be bigger, stronger, wiser, and kind. The way you parent your child must be a mixture of firm and kind styles of parenting. You must teach your child about boundaries as well as empathy.

Self-reflection

Spend some time by yourself daily. Set a couple of minutes aside for self-reflection. The only way you can work on improving yourself is through self-reflection. It will help you understand the areas where you are doing well and the ones where you must improve. It also gives you a chance to understand your parenting style.

The three things you must keep in mind when it comes to self-reflection are as follows. You must try and make sense of your own emotions, feelings, thoughts, and behaviors. Make a note of all the different areas of parenting you would want to improve. Start journaling all these things. Finally, talk to someone you trust about all these things and start working through your list of concerns. Take things one day at a time, and don't be in a rush.

Seek Help

When it comes to parenting, there is no instruction manual to follow. All you need to do is keep trying and then trying some more until you figure out a style of parenting that works well for you as well as you can. It takes plenty of time and effort to do this. Parenting is a process of trial and error, and once you understand this, it becomes easier. At times, you might not have the emotional skills required to deal with certain situations as a parent. If this seems to be the case for you, it is all right. It is okay to need a little help from time to time. Don't be ashamed, and don't hesitate to ask for help. If you feel like meeting the demands of parenthood is becoming extremely overwhelming, if you're worried about your reactions, or just want to learn about ways in which you can strengthen your bond with your child, then seek professional help. Talking to a counselor, psychologist, or even a relationship therapist can be quite helpful. The only thing you must remember is that it is okay to ask for help.

This isn't something you can achieve overnight, and it takes consistent effort, time, and patience. Even if it sounds like hard work, you must power through. By incorporating the different tips given mentioned above, you will feel more confident and self-assured. Once your child picks up these positive vibes from you, he will start modeling this behavior. When it comes to parenting, I believe that the saying, "Always lead by example," makes perfect sense.

If you want to teach your child about self-love, he must see this in your behavior. The simplest way to promote such a positive attitude is by celebrating life and celebrating yourself. Whenever you accomplish any of your goals in life, learn to celebrate. Rejoice in all the victories that come your way and learn to carry on even after you run into obstacles. As a parent, you are your child's first-ever role model. I know it might sound a little stressful, but to your child, you are their superhero!

NOTES:

CHAPTER 2

Set Aside Time When You Give Them Undivided Attention

Time management is one of the essential skills required in life. By learning to manage your time effectively, you can ensure that you're concentrating on productive and crucial tasks. Time management also teaches you the importance of prioritizing different aspects of your life. If this skill is so important, then why do so many people struggle with it? Well, time is a finite resource, even if it seems like you have your whole life ahead of you, the time you have in your hand is always fixed. Even if you wish for it, there will only be 24 hours in a day. Since time is fixed, you must decide how to spend it wisely. According to me, there is no sin greater than squandering away one's time. The time that is lost can never come back. Therefore, learning to manage your time is essential.

I am sure you are wondering what time management has got to do with raising a child? That said, it doesn't mean you give up on your other jobs and responsibilities just because you chose parenthood. You will need to learn to balance your professional and personal lives while being a good parent to your little one. If you end up sacrificing one aspect of your life for another, it will only bog you down in the end. For instance, if you keep sacrificing your social life for your child's schedule, there will come a time when you'll be extremely frustrated with yourself and your kid too. Avoid this to prevent a potential burnout. Hence you must learn to manage your time effectively.

Children love attention, and this is one of the best ways to strengthen a parent-child bond. Your child loves being the center of your attention. I realized that most of the tantrums my kids threw while growing up were all because they wanted my attention. When you give your child attention, it must be undivided. Simply put, your child must be your only focus and nothing else. When it comes to spending time with your child, quality matters more than quantity. Your child will be happier if you spend 30 minutes playing catch instead of spending three meaningless hours together where you keep glancing at your phone.

Being good at time management is one of the most important skills of parenthood. As a mother of four kids, I truly understand how difficult it might be to manage your time along with everything else you have to do. The key is to provide your kid with sufficient attention without going overboard. If you smother your child with attention or give no attention whatsoever, it will negatively affect his mental and emotional growth. Therefore, concentrate on having meaningful interactions with your kid.

For the sake of his healthy development, it is essential that you provide him focused attention. I'm not suggesting that you must pay attention to him every waking minute of the day but provide attention regularly and daily. If you keep fussing behind your child every single minute of the day, he will assume that he is entitled to attention whenever he desires. This, in turn, will instill a sense of entitlement in him. To avoid this, start concentrating on the quality of time you spend with him.

In the next section, you'll learn about the ways in which you can begin spending quality time with your child and give him the attention that is important for his healthy development.

Small Installments

A lot of parents don't understand the meaning of spending quality time with their kids. This is becoming a great hurdle, especially in this modern age of distraction and technology. Parenting is a full-time job, unlike a nine-to-five desk job. Your responsibilities don't start at nine in the morning and end at five in the evening. Instead of setting aside two hours to spend with your kid, start breaking it up into smaller installments. Spending time with your child is not a client meeting. Don't think that it will take up a significant chunk of your day, but think of it as an enjoyable activity.

Children, especially the young ones, have a very short attention span. They get easily distracted by things around them and can't concentrate on anything for more than a couple of minutes at a stretch. Start using this to your advantage. If you have a young child at home, consider giving him attention in intervals. It is not only an excellent way to engage with him, but it also works well with his ability to pay attention. For every hour that you're awake, try spending about six to 10 minutes focusing on your child. Eventually, it will add up to the same amount of time, but it will become more enjoyable for your kid as well as you. Spending time with your child is not a chore. When you give your child quality time and focused attention, you are strengthening the bond you share with him.

No Gadgets

If you continuously check your emails or if your phone keeps beeping constantly, how can you spend quality time with your kids? The quality of the interactions you have with your child will considerably reduce when you try to multitask. Your child must not have to compete with your smartphone to get your attention. After all, it is their right to have your undivided attention, and it is your responsibility to provide them with it, as humanly as possible. It is not that difficult, and it helps you strengthen and nurture the parent-child bond.

You merely need to keep your smartphone or any other gadgets away whenever you spend time with your child. For instance, if you're reading a story to your kid, ensure that there are no distractions in the room. Switch off the TV, turn off the music, keep your gadgets away, and concentrate only on the story and your child. This is an excellent way for you to detach from the stressors of your daily life. Apart from this, it will also make your child feel like he is the center of your attention. Getting rid of distractions when you're spending time with your child is the simplest way to spend meaningful time with your little one. Don't try to multitask; concentrate only on one task at a time. This is also a great way to teach your child about good habits while conversing with others.

Contact Matters

You must maintain eye contact with your child whenever you are spending time with him. Not just that, also include physical contact with him. It can be something as simple as holding his hand once in a while, giving him a peck on his cheek, or even a quick hug. All these tiny gestures are great ways to display your affection. It will make your child feel like he belongs and he is loved.

For instance, if you are playing with your child, tickle them a bit. Not only will he feel important, even you'll feel quite delighted when he starts giggling and laughing. It is a great way to bond with your child. All the physical gestures of showing your love will teach your child about the expression of love. By maintaining eye contact, you're showing him that you are concentrating on spending time with him and on whatever he is saying. Listen attentively to him and don't interrupt him whenever he is talking to you.

Separation

If you have more than one child at home, then you must allocate separate time for each of your children. No, I'm not suggesting that you use the divide and conquer technique. I'm merely saying that the attention you provide each child must be easily differentiable. For instance, don't put all your children in one room and spend 20 minutes with them. This doesn't qualify as quality one-on-one time. Instead, spend time with each of your kids. Your child must not think that he has to compete with his sibling for your attention. That being said, it is also important to spend time together as a family too. It shows your child that you truly love him and that you are more than happy to spend time with him. If you don't spend sufficient time with him, it can put a strain on your relationship.

Also, if any of your children feel like you are spending all your time with only one of them, sibling jealousy and rivalry will creep in. These undesirable emotions will put a strain on the bond your child shares with his siblings.

Identify Positive Behavior

Even when you can't set aside time for meaningful interactions with your little one, always look out for any surprising positive behaviors. Think of these as behavioral Easter eggs. Behavioral Easter eggs often include certain positives instead of negative actions that you want to see in your child. Whenever your child behaves the way you expect him to, it is time to validate his efforts and praise him for the same. It's almost similar to a mini treasure hunt you set for yourself.

Regardless of whether it is playtime or not, if you see something that you truly appreciate about your child, then show your appreciation. For instance, if your child is not a big fan of sharing his playthings with others, and you notice that he is sharing his favorite toy with his friend, then it is time to show some appreciation. You don't have to reward him in any big way, but a simple hug will also help. If you notice any positive behavior, immediately compliment the child for the same. Positive reinforcement is the best way to teach good behavior to young children. Not just children, positive reinforcement works even with adults. If someone praises you for doing something well, wouldn't you repeat the same behavior in the future to attain their praise again? Likewise, even your child will do the same.

One thing I wish I had known sooner as a parent is related to balancing time with kids. You must learn to leave your child alone when you're supposed to, and then spend time with him wherever you can. It is perfectly all right to alternate between fully engaging with your child and then entirely ignoring them. This is much better than paying half attention to him and concentrating on something else. Giving your child 10 minutes of complete attention is better than spending 30 minutes sitting beside him while checking your emails.

For instance, if you work from home, then using this all-or-nothing approach will work wonders. Just because you are at home doesn't mean that you have to spend every single minute with your child. It cannot be clubbed under harsh parenting. It is merely about getting your things done without compromising on the attention you give your child. It also teaches your child that he is not supposed to disturb mommy or daddy when they are working. When your child knows what he is supposed to do and not do, it becomes easier to regulate his expectations. Parenting must not prevent you from getting your work done. Likewise, other things must not stop you from being a good parent to your child. Learn to pay attention and balance your time with your child by effectively managing your time.

NOTES:

_____

_____

_____

_____

_____

_____

_____

_____

_____

_____

_____

_____

_____

CHAPTER 3

Resist Comparing Them to Others

Competition is important for growth. Only when you compete with others will you know how well you are doing or learn where you lag. We live in a highly competitive world. In fact, you'll seldom find any area of life where there is no competition. On the downside, the competition seems to have spread its hold into every aspect of life, and therefore it is essential to teach your child the importance of staying grounded. If you keep comparing your child with others, it will prove detrimental. It is natural human nature to compare. However, if you constantly compare your child with another child or even his sibling, it is not conducive towards his positive development. Instead, teach your child to be a better version of himself. Show him that he doesn't have to be better than others but try to teach him to explore his full potential. In the words of Mark Twain, *"Comparison is the thief of joy."*

Think of a scenario where you look at a well-behaved child at a restaurant who is sitting in his highchair and eating carefully. Now, you turn your attention to your child and see that he is flinging spaghetti across the table and is spilling food everywhere. What would you think of such a situation? You would naturally wish that your child were better behaved. You might even mentally compare him to the other child. Thoughts like these might prompt you to express such a comparison verbally.

When this happens, you may end up using words or phrases such as "Why can't you be more like ____?" or "Look at her, she is doing so much better than you!" As hard as you try to refrain yourself from doing this, you might end up doing it at one point of time or the other. It is an inevitable trait of human nature and is an impulse that very few people can suppress. Healthy competition is essential, but comparison seldom works. I believe that comparison is counter-productive, not just for children, but even for adults.

Children are quite tender, and they lack the mental maturity to accept criticism positively. After all, even adults struggle with accepting criticism, how can you expect a child to do that? This criticism is even more stinging for a child when you start comparing him with others. If you constantly tell your child that others are better than him, it will make him feel unappreciated and unloved. I'm not saying that you must never correct your child when he is going wrong, I'm merely saying that you must refrain from making unnecessary comparisons. There are ways to teach your child to be better, but comparison is not among this list.

I have four kids to look after, and each of them is different. If one child is good at something, it doesn't necessarily mean I expect the same from all my children. This is what parenting has taught me. I need to learn to manage my expectations while giving my child all the tools he requires to become a better version of himself. To be honest, there have been instances when I compared my children with others mentally. However, instead of doing this, I realized that as a parent, it is my responsibility to teach my child to be better.

Harmful Effects Of Comparison

Every human being is unique, and every child is unique. If you continuously harangue your child about how much better others are than him, it will develop an unnecessary inferiority complex in them. This, in turn, will hurt his overall mental development. Not just this, even his self-esteem will take a beating. In this section, let us look at the adverse effect comparison can have on your child. Once you go through this list, I am certain that you will think twice before you say something like, "Why can't you be like ____?"

Trigger self-doubt

If someone repeatedly tells you that you're not good enough or that others are much better than you, what will happen to your self-confidence? Well, you will obviously start doubting yourself. Even more so, if this sort of criticism comes from someone you hold dear. If comparison can be this harmful for an adult, it is extremely harmful for a child.

Jealousy

Refrain from comparing your child with his siblings, his peers, your neighbors, his cousins, or anyone else. Once he starts harboring jealousy, it will quickly turn into other undesirable emotions like aggression, hatred, and he might even start resenting others.

Discontentment

As a parent, if you keep comparing your child with others, you might start believing that your child is not good enough. You might even think that others are much better than him. You would probably start to doubt your own parenting skills. It is okay to want your child to excel, but when you start comparing him to others, you are merely making him question his own abilities. You might start questioning your skills as a parent too. You would think that you are going wrong somewhere because of which your child is not doing better. Well, trust me, this kind of thinking is a recipe for disaster.

Negativity seeps in

Comparison breeds negativity. He will feel as if nothing matters, no matter what he does, he can never measure up to others and that he will always be left behind. If he starts feeling like this, he will give up. Why must he even make an effort when he can never measure up?

Relationship

Constant comparison will take a toll on the bond you share with your child. If you keep telling your child that others are better than him, he will eventually start harboring feelings of resentment towards you. He might believe that he can never please you or make you happy. Even if your criticism stems from the concern of his overall well-being, it will still seem like stinging criticism to him. He cannot see your positive intentions, and it will put an unnecessary strain on the bond you share with him.

Adulthood

All the criticism that you dole out to your child during his childhood will stay with him once he enters adulthood too. Don't be surprised if he turns into a perpetually nervous and jittery adult. Instead of trying to make himself better, all his attention will be focused on making you feel better. This is not a sign of positive growth. If he starts feeling that he can never meet your expectations, it will naturally harm his self-confidence.

Unnecessary stress

Childhood is all about growth and development. A child's focus must be on understanding himself and his skills. He must be given the freedom to explore the world around him and the world within him. If you subject him to constant comparison, he will forget about all this, and will instead concentrate on doing better to gain your approval merely. It will leave him feeling quite tired, drained out, and even exhausted. This kind of exhaustion at a young age is not suitable for his overall health. Not a lot of adults can successfully handle stress. Imagine how much more difficult it would be for a young child to handle this kind of stress?

Withdrawal

Eventually, your child will get tired of this comparison and will start withdrawing himself. He will start believing that regardless of all that he does, he can never be better than others or even match their performance. He will ultimately give up and might not even try to attempt things.

Positive Attitude Instead of Comparing

Raising your child without comparing him to others might be a little tricky, but it is certainly possible. The key to making this change is slightly tweaking your attitude and outlook toward life. Instead of comparing him to others, encourage him to do better, concentrate on his strengths, and always celebrate his accomplishments.

As a parent of four kids, I know that all my kids are completely different from one another. They might have certain similarities, but they have plenty of differences too. These differences make them special and unique. Instead of comparing your child with someone else, why don't you embrace his originality? Before you learn to stop comparing your child with others, you must understand why you usually compare.

Regardless of whether it is a single parent, a joint family, or even a two-parent household, it is essential to ensure that your parental mindset is clear and full of confidence. The urge to compare can sneak in whenever it wants to. Usually, parents tend to compare their kids with not just others' children, but also their peers as well as cousins. So, why do parents compare? Well, we compare it because it is the human tendency to compare. In fact, I believe that it has been wired into our biological system. The human brain is always trying to sort things out, solve a problem, and, unfortunately, comparison happens to be a technique that most of us use while making decisions. It might not seem like much to you, but the comparison does leave an everlasting impact on your child's psyche. Now let's talk about how we, as parents, can prevent comparison.

Awareness

Your body language and the words you use matter a lot. Your kid isn't as naive as you think he is. He can understand when you are genuine and when you are not. Most of these silent messages that he keeps receiving are sent from you unknowingly. For instance, I remember this scene where I was at one of my son's football games at his school and there was a dad on the football field who kept cheering on his son's best friend. Instead of cheering on his son, he kept cheering on another kid who went on to score the winning goal. At the end of the game, this dad goes to his kid and praises him by saying, "good game Jake." However, Jake knew that the praise he received from his father was not genuine and it was an empty praise. He knows this because his father cheered on for his best friend and not him.

So, what did you learn from this example? The lesson to learn is that you need to be conscious of your behavior whenever you are around your child and his peers. If one of your child's friends does better than your own kid, then offer praise, but don't compare. At times, whenever you feel like the bug of comparison is sneaking into your mind, take a pause. Take a moment to yourself and redirect your thoughts. Instead, concentrate on all the good that your kid did!

Energy matters

You might have probably noticed that your child is an energy sponge. The kind of energy you generate is the same kind of energy your child seems to display. The type of energy you give out often resonates with the kind of energy your child experiences and gives out. If you notice that one of your children is more outgoing than the other, then it is natural that you will be more drawn to the child who shares the kind of energy that you do. This, in turn, might make the quieter child feel like you don't want to spend much time with him. So, it is time that you start treating each of your children as different entities. The way you deal with one child might not work for the other. Therefore, you need to personalize the approach you adopt and talk to them in such a manner that appeals to them. Understand the child and then devise a plan of action to deal with him.

Accomplishments

If your child overhears you gush to another adult about your pride in someone else's achievements, it will hurt your child's self-confidence. Parents, please listen up! It is okay to praise other kids, but don't get carried away. Learn to compliment your child, offer genuine praise, and help him become his best self. Don't compare him to others, he is different, and so are you. Also, whenever you are talking about your child, avoid using generic phrases. If you have just praised another child for two minutes and then end the conversation with something about your child by saying something along the lines of, "Yeah, he is good," it will hurt your child. Think of three things that you truly appreciate about your child and remind yourself about these things. Not just yourself, but even bring these up while conversing with others. When your child knows that you are proud of him and his efforts, he will strive to do well.

Replacement of phrases

You might see a well-behaved child at a checkout counter and then look down at your own kid who seems to be having a temper tantrum. In such an instance, you might ask him, "Why can't you be more like him?" this kind of comparison often stings, even more so if your child actually knows the other kid you are comparing him to. When you make such statements, you make your child believe that you would rather have the other kid instead of him. Instead of saying, "Why can't you be more like ___?" replace it with "I am so proud of you/your ____!" Learn to celebrate your child's individuality.

Instead of resorting to comparison, set some benchmarks. Start appreciating the effort your child makes, even if it doesn't seem significant, offer genuine appreciation. This helps develop his self-confidence. If you think your child requires a little extra support, then give him the strength required to overcome any of his weaknesses. Always support him and allow him to understand that you will be there for him. Don't just focus on his weaknesses, praise him for his strengths too. Don't force your child to do something he doesn't like. It will only add to his frustrations. Allow your child to explore his strengths and interests. Apart from all this, provide him with unconditional love and support.

Everyone deals with peer pressure at different stages of life. Peer pressure is not just limited to childhood or teenage years. In fact, parents are quite susceptible to giving in to peer pressure. This usually shows up in the form of competition or comparison. Never force your child to do something merely because someone else seems to be doing it. Don't force your kid to learn the cello. If he doesn't like it, he might be more interested in learning to play basketball. As a parent, it is your duty to provide your child with the necessary support and encouragement he requires to discover his preferences. Give him the space required to pursue his interests. Once he does this, his chances of being successful in his field of interest will increase.

A common mistake that a lot of parents tend to make is that they tend to associate their self-esteem as a parent with their child's performance. You might love your child dearly, and he might feel like he's an extension of your body, but keep in mind that he is a separate entity. You are not your child, and your self-esteem doesn't depend on the way your child performs. Whenever you push your child to do something he doesn't want, you are preventing him from excelling in what he wants. If your child starts complaining that you always take someone else's side or that you keep comparing him to others, then it is probably time that you pay attention to the nonverbal and verbal actions you display.

Try practicing each of these tips and make a note of your observations in the journal. It will help you analyze which methods work the best with your kid.

It would do you good to remember that perfection is nothing more than an illusion. You will never attain perfection even if you keep chasing it all your life. Although you can try to excel in whatever you choose. Don't expect perfection from yourself or from your child. Everyone has to face different challenges, and each challenge will be different. No two children are alike, and no two parents are similar. So, save yourself and your child from a world of trouble by preventing yourself from making any unnecessary comparisons.

NOTES:

_____

_____

_____

_____

_____

_____

_____

_____

_____

_____

_____

_____

_____

_____

CHAPTER 4

Ensure They Know Your Love Is Unconditional

Secrets to Loving Your Child Unconditionally

Unconditional love is given without expecting anything in return. It has the ability to love someone, regardless of what they do or say. It is the kind of love that will never fail and will always stay. The simplest example of unconditional love is the one between a parent and a child. We all acknowledge the fact that children require unconditional love. Usually, most parents do love their children unconditionally. After all, regardless of how irritated we all tend to get with our kids, we can say that we could go to any extent to save a child's life. One of my teenagers was rather troublesome growing up. From being a mama's boy, he went to become a complete rebel within a few years. God knows I tried to be patient with him, but there were instances when I used to lose my cool. In fact, it almost seemed like he was trying everything he possibly could to push my buttons. Even after all that, I know that if my child needs any help or that if he is in danger, I will go to any extent to protect him. This stands true for all parents. The minute we enter into adulthood, there occurs a simple change in our biology. Our parental instincts kick in. The survival of a child becomes more important than our own survival.

Are you thinking what has all this got to do with parenting? You must not only love your child but must also know how to express this love to your child. Another simple factor you must take into consideration is how your child feels. If your child doesn't know that you love him unconditionally, then there are a couple of changes you are required to make. Grab your journal, make note of the following questions and carefully answer them.

- Does your child know that he is extremely lovable the way he is?
- Does he know that you don't expect him to be perfect?

- Does he know that any emotions he experiences are a part of growing up and that he can always count on you to help him manage those emotions?
- Does he know that he will never have to do anything or pretend to be someone else to gain your love?

You might have never thought about these things consciously, and I'm sure you're thinking about them now. How can you teach a child all these things? Well, the answer is much easier than you think. You love your child unconditionally, even when he is driving you mad.

Here are a couple of situations you must consider.

There will be instances when you need to set certain boundaries. Love your kid and stay connected with him even as you enforce these boundaries. By doing this, he will effectively learn that he is not a bad person and that whatever he's doing just makes him human.

Think of a situation where your child breaks your favorite dinner plate. It is justified that you will get angry at that. Instead of lashing out at him, regardless of how justified your anger is, calmly talk to him about the problem. By doing this, you are setting a good role model of how he is supposed to handle his emotions. He will learn to regulate and manage any strong emotions he experiences by copying your behavior.

Whenever you're setting boundaries or limits, you must empathize with him. Instead of forcing him to listen to you, tell him that you understand him. By doing this, he will want to follow the limits you are setting. This will teach him self-discipline.

Keep in mind that your child is still a child. He isn't completely mature and lacks the understanding to differentiate right from wrong. Therefore, he will make mistakes. It is your responsibility to teach him that making mistakes is okay as long as he learns from those mistakes. Teach him that mistakes are a simple part of growing up, and this experience cannot be eliminated from his life.

Whenever you make a mistake, don't forget to apologize. This will make him understand responsibility and ownership of his actions. He will learn that he is supposed to deal with his emotions, and he is responsible for what he feels. Apart from this, it teaches him to clean up his messes.

Always accept your child for who he is and don't compare him to others. Help your child to be his best self. By doing this, he will learn that he is good enough the way he is.

Woah, does all this seem like a little too much? Here are five simple tips you can follow to love your child unconditionally.

Feelings vs. Behaviors

It is essential to distinguish between feelings and actions. The emotions or feelings your child experiences are never wrong or bad. However, certain behaviors can be easily categorized as being unreasonable. By distinguishing between these two, you can teach a great deal about unconditional love to your child. The practical application of unconditional love often comes in the form of empathy. Your child feels that he is understood as well as accepted when you express empathy. He will feel these things even when you implement certain limits. You must try to reconnect, empathize, and also invite him to talk about the deeper feelings fueling his actions. You can say something like, "You're probably quite upset to talk to me. Honey, what is going on?"

Patiently listen to what your child says. Take a couple of deep breaths or count to ten and calm yourself down. You are supposed to teach your child about emotional intelligence while you are setting certain limits. If your child is throwing a temper tantrum, then instead of scolding him, ask him what went wrong. While doing this, you must show empathy. You can say something along the lines of, "You are disappointed that we could not stay longer and eat ice cream at the restaurant, is that it?" Remember, whenever you're empathizing with his anger, you are not validating his undesirable behavior. Merely because you understand what he is doing to fulfill his needs doesn't mean that you have to meet his needs. For instance, a little empathy and love from you might help take the disappointment away from the fact that he doesn't get to eat ice cream.

A common misunderstanding a lot of parents have is they believe that empathy is synonymous with allowing poor behavior. If your child is misbehaving, it is your duty and responsibility to correct his behavior. You don't have to do this immediately but can do this later when everyone is calmer. When you know your child is quiet and will listen to you, start reinforcing the necessary limits and talk to him about how he can deal with such situations in the future. He might become upset when his friend knocks down his tower of building blocks. This might have prompted him to shove his friend. You are supposed to condemn such behavior, but at the same time, you're also supposed to teach him how he can handle any extreme emotions he experiences. So, it is time to have a one-on-one talk with your little one. Tell him that you understand why he is upset, but at the same time also tell him that he's not supposed to lash out at others. Tell him that his friends are there for him to have some fun and nothing else. Ask him what he would like to do the next time he gets upset? He might have a couple of suggestions, and if he doesn't, you can give him some ideas. Maybe you can encourage him to tell his friend not to knock down his tower and be careful when playing. Maybe he can tell the friend to behave well, as his actions upset him. Once you come up with a list of suggestions and answers, it is time to start practicing them.

Child's Perspective

All parents tend to believe that they are always right. This means they think that their child is wrong. Well, this means you believe that if you are correct, it means the other person is wrong. This isn't necessarily true. There are various perspectives from which a situation can be viewed. What might seem wrong to you from your perspective might seem right to your child from his viewpoint. So, by merely changing your perspective, you might be able to understand your child better. Whenever your child is misbehaving, don't get upset, even if every fiber of your being is prompting you to discipline him. If your child is doing something which might harm him, stop him from doing it, and stay calm. Whenever your child misbehaves, there's always a reason which has led to it. It can stem from any feelings of being upset or even an unfulfilled need. You must try to address the underlying cause and try to solve or address the feeling he's experiencing. By addressing the underlying feeling, you can effectively fix any wrong behavior he displays. Think of his misbehavior as a blatant SOS he is giving out; it is time you respond to it.

Maybe your child would be nicer to his friend if they could both play with his toys. Or maybe your child lashes out because he is uncomfortable with the idea of sharing. If you teach him to share and encourage such behavior, he will soon get the hang of it. Maybe he would not shout if he knows that you are listening to him. Usually, children tend to yell or raise their volume when they feel unheard. Maybe he would be kinder to his younger sibling if he was not upset that he lost his unique place in the household. His display of poor behavior might also be a scream for attention. He might just want your love and attention because he is not getting enough.

Whenever children start to act out, they are effectively telling us in the only way they possibly know that they need our help. As a parent, it is your responsibility to understand what your child is trying to tell you. If your child still doesn't have the vocabulary to express himself easily, he will try expressing himself in any way he possibly can. It might mean temper tantrums or even crying. Whenever these things happen, don't lose your cool. You are the adult in this equation, and you must be calm. If you start reacting emotionally, the entire situation will become extremely volatile. Take a moment, step back from the situation, and try to see it from your child's perspective. His misbehavior might become understandable to you, and you might have the "aha!" moment where you figure out what went wrong. Any obstacle to love will fade away, and your words will become truly unconditional.

Appreciation

Learn to appreciate your child and stop trying to change him into someone he isn't. Think of your child as a flower. You might not get to choose the kind of flower he is, but you can certainly provide him a nurturing environment that helps him fully blossom. If you wish that your child behaves like someone else or if you're trying to change your child, then your child will quickly catch on. Children are a little naive, but they are really good at sensing any changes in their parent's behavior.

He might not understand what you're trying to do or might not even be able to express it verbally, but he will undoubtedly sense it. He will probably start to think that the way he is isn't good enough for you or that he isn't lovable.

When it comes to his development, self-confidence is essential. You might not realize it, but when you take pride in him and are delighted by whatever he does, he will be filled with a sense of self-confidence. Every child requires appreciation. You must provide this appreciation daily and ensure that it is genuine. If you realize that you're having a rather tough time doing this, then maybe it is time for a little self-introspection. Probably some grief from your past is holding you back from unconditionally loving your child. Or perhaps you have some resentment towards your child because he isn't all that you wished for.

Once you acknowledge these feelings, it becomes easier to process and deal with them. Never try to bury or ignore such powerful feelings because they can easily translate into visible resentment towards your child. You are allowed to feel whatever you experience. don't be ashamed of them. Once you identify the emotion, you can efficiently work on the underlying cause of such emotion. When you address the underlying issue, it becomes easier to deal with your emotions. If you want to love your child and appreciate him unconditionally, then you must take responsibility for all your emotions.

Once you do this, it is time to change your perspective towards your child. If you notice that a plant is wilting, what would you do? Would you yell at the plant to get better, or will you provide the care and nourishment it requires to grow stronger? You would definitely provide it the nourishment it requires. Likewise, you're supposed to be nourishing and caring towards your child as well. When your child knows that you love him unconditionally, that he can depend on you for anything, and that you will always have his back, he will flourish and thrive. Positive feelings from his parents will fill the child with the confidence required to keep going in life.

Empathy Instead of Punishment
The love a child feels is often withdrawn whenever he is punished. If the child is physically punished, regardless of what you tell him, he will not feel like he is loved. He will still perceive any consequences that you impose on him, which are based on his actions, as being an intentional means to inflict pain upon him. The child who is punished might not fully comprehend the reasons why he is punished unless the reasons are

explained to him. Until then, he will feel like his parents are intentionally hurting him. So, it is not surprising that a child who is continuously punished feels unloved and unwanted.

That said, I'm not suggesting that you must never correct your child if he goes wrong or makes a mistake. It is your duty to correct him whenever he goes wrong. However, there is a proper way to do it. You must not be harsh, and at the same time, you must not be too easy-going either. You need to strike a balance between the two. There are various techniques that are used for punishment, but most of these techniques fail to explain the reason why the child is being punished. For instance, if you withhold your expression of love towards the child because he misbehaves, he will come to the conclusion that the love given to him can be withdrawn at any moment. Well, I'm sure this is not the lesson you want your kid to learn. Instead, if you sit down with your child and explain what he's supposed to and not supposed to do, it will make more sense. Spend time connecting with your child, setting limits, and explaining why the limits are set. By doing this, you're encouraging the development of emotional intelligence in your kid as well as morality. When this happens, your child's want to do the right thing and behave properly will stem from an inherent desire and not an external motivation. Whenever you follow any of the tips mentioned up until now, it is time to journalize. Write in detail about the incident, your response or reaction to it, along with any changes you would want to make.

A Little Faith

Have a little faith that once your child knows that he is unconditionally loved, he is capable of changing his behavior. What if your child misbehaves and crosses a limit? You are required to be brave. You must not accept defeat, and neither must you give in to your fears. Don't give up on your child, but instead, bring him back. Welcome him into a loving embrace and allow him to understand that he is loved unconditionally. When you start loving your child unconditionally, you're showing him that you believe in his inherent goodness. This, in turn, will strengthen his belief in himself, and he will start trusting you as well. So, by showing unconditional love, you can help a child who feels disconnected with the present. Unconditional love is a potent tool, and when you know how to express it, the bond you share with your little one can never be destroyed.

Yes, it certainly takes some time, consistent effort, and motivation. However, the rewards it offers will certainly make all your efforts worthwhile. By following these simple habits, you can strengthen the bond you share with your child. Apart from this, it will also help improve his behavior and set the tone for the rest of his life. When he starts believing that he is good enough the way he is and is loved exactly as he is, he will blossom into a wonderful adult.

Expression of Unconditional Love

Growing up, I used to listen to crazy stories about all the fun my mother had in her childhood. She usually shared stories that used to make me laugh until my tummy hurt. However, one fine day, she told me that she was sent to boarding school at a very young age. At this, I excitedly mentioned that she was quite lucky to receive an excellent education the way she did. Suddenly, she looked rather sad and said, "I don't think parents would send their kids away if they love them." This simple statement made by her shocked me to my very core. I never realized that my mother felt unloved by her parents. This confession made by her was a verbal expression of the emotional wounds she tended all her life. Even if her parents loved her, they failed to express it to her. This is what made me realize that unconditionally loving your child is one part of the equation. The other part of the equation is being able to express this love. You might have all the love in the world for your child, but it doesn't serve any purpose if you fail to express this love to him. Love doesn't necessarily have to be expressed verbally, but it can also be conveyed through gestures and actions.Let us look at some simple ways in which you can start expressing your unconditional love to your child.

You are supposed to love your child unconditionally and you cannot express that love if you don't feel it. There will be moments when your child's behavior will test your patience. However, unconditional love must prevail even during such circumstances. Maybe after a very long and tiring day, you come back home and notice that your son's room is as messy as it was the day earlier. He probably promised to clean it up and failed to keep up his promise. Maybe one of your kids sneaks out, breaks curfew, and comes back early in the morning. Or maybe one of your kids barely manages to pass a subject at school. Regardless of what the situation is, you are supposed to love your child unconditionally. There must be no limits to it, and there are no conditions applicable.

There is only so much time that you have, and there are plenty of things you can do with the time available. Therefore, it is important that you don't squander the time available to you. More than anything else in this world, your child desires your love and attention. So, ensure that you spend as much time with your child as you possibly can. While you spend time with him, make sure that you concentrate only on your child and nothing else during this period. You can always attend your work later, but for now, spend time with your little one. Trust me, time flies by, especially when you're a parent. Within no time, your child will go from being your little bundle of joy to an adult man or woman making their way in the real world. Time flies by; if you don't make the most of it, it will all be gone within the blink of an eye.

As a parent, you will not only have to make some tough decisions but will also have to play the role of a bad cop from time to time. Don't shy away from all such situations. It is a part of your duty as a parent. You are supposed to do the right thing and stand by your decision. Your child might be upset because of all this, but trust your decisions. One fine day, your child will realize that everything you did was for his own benefit. The love that you show toward your child will reflect when he is an adult.

You can truly get you to know your child only when you spend time with him. Try to understand what he likes and dislikes. Learn to identify his triggers and the things that make him tick. Observe what he is passionate about and what his interests are. Once you do all this, you can provide the required support and motivation to pursue his passions. A common fear all children have is that they will end up disappointing their parents. Ensure that your child knows that he can never do this. The only way you can convey this message is by being his pillar of strength. Your child must understand that he can always rely on you, regardless of how bad things turn out to be.

If you love anything about your child, then tell him about it. It is not just merely about loving your child, explaining your reasons for loving him will help improve his self-image. Make it a point to tell your child that you love him and do so regularly. Apart from this, from time to time, ensure that you tell him that he makes you proud.

Affection must be conveyed through words as well as actions. Hug your kid, kiss him, and hold his hand. Some people aren't comfortable with physical expressions of love and tend to shy away from these things. Well, if that's the case with you, then work on overcoming this hesitation. A warm hug can lift his spirits when he is feeling blue.

Also, these physical gestures of affection will make you feel better too.

You must learn to celebrate your child. After all, if the parent doesn't celebrate, who else would? There will be different milestones in your child's life, including his birthdays, school graduation, or even recitals. Start celebrating all these milestones. As I've mentioned, the time that passes by will never return. Therefore, make the most of it and learn to cherish the time you have with your child. Make a big deal of these events; make your child feel special.

You might not realize it, but your child notices everything you do. Most of the behaviors they learn are usually the behaviors they see the parents make. The way you behave sets precedence for the way your child will behave. So, be a role model and a good one at that. Apart from this, spend time with your child and share everything you know. If you're good at playing basketball, teach him to play basketball. This can be an activity you and your child can do together. If you are good at baking, then have your child help you in the kitchen, he can be your sous chef! Find some activities you can teach your child, and then use them as a means to strengthen the bond you share with him. Whenever you are teaching something new, you are required to be patient.

Learn to let go. This is perhaps one aspect where a lot of parents struggle. Once you have equipped your kid with everything he needs, you are supposed to give him the freedom to explore the world around him. Don't place unnecessary restrictions, implement only those limits which are essential for his well being. Trust him and respect his boundaries. Have little faith that you have taught him well and that he knows the difference between right and wrong. Give him the support he requires and show him that you love him unconditionally.

NOTES:

_____

_____

_____

_____

_____

_____

_____

_____

_____

_____

_____

_____

CHAPTER 5

Encourage Them To Try New Things To Develop New Skills

Strategies and Activities

A child who lacks self-confidence will often shy away from trying a new activity or even learning a new skill. Apart from this, such a child will be quite hesitant when faced with challenges, and he might also be afraid of tackling any obstacles that come along his way. As a parent, it is your responsibility to encourage your child to try out different activities in life. If he doesn't try, he will never know what he likes and dislikes. To ensure that he takes the first step and tries something, you're supposed to give him the confidence required to do so. Usually, different factors might scare the child or seem overwhelming at first. Children are worried that they'll end up disappointing their parents or are scared of failure. Both these things can be quite crippling in an adult and are even more overwhelming for a child.

Time for a little confession, I used to be quite scared of trying new things, especially during my childhood. If I felt that I wasn't good at something, I refused to do it. I used to partake in only those activities wherein I was confident that I would excel. If I didn't think this was the case, then I usually avoided such activities. Then came parenthood. When I started to see my little ones express fear and apprehension like I used to, it didn't feel right. I wanted my children to try different activities and skills. I wanted them to explore all this to determine their abilities, skills, and preferences. I didn't want my children to tell me, "Mommy, I cannot do this," or "Mommy, this isn't for me." That's when I realized the crippling effect of fear.

Fear is a widespread emotion and is quite powerful. Whenever you face a new experience or even come across a challenge, your body's response to it is in the form of fear. Such circumstances often make kids feel vulnerable, powerless, and anxious. It takes away their sense of security as well as control. Because of all this, kids are often hesitant when they have to try something new and prefer avoiding all that's unfamiliar. Instead of experiencing these unpleasant emotions, children usually prefer not to attempt anything new. It, in turn, often leads to missed opportunities because the child was too scared to try. This same negative pattern of thinking is likely to follow your child into his adulthood as well. If you want your child to become a confident adult who doesn't hesitate, then it is time you break the pattern of fear. How will your kid know whether he is good or not good at something unless he tries it? To try something, he needs to let go of his fear and anxiety. There have been times when you wondered about all the things you probably missed out on because you were too scared to try them. This regret wasn't something I wanted my children to experience once they grow up. Therefore, I decided it was time to help build my child's confidence so that he could face the world fearlessly. You will now learn about the different strategies you can use to help develop your child's confidence as well as enthusiasm to try new things. These strategies are quite simple, make a note of them in your parenting journal. Review them once in a while and these ideas will stay embedded in your subconscious.

Being Supportive

There are different reasons why a child might be scared of trying new things. Factors include a child's past experiences, his state of mind, the environment he is used to, and his upbringing. This kind of fear is also rather common among children who have received praise from the primary caregivers only when they have succeeded. For instance, if a child gets approval only when he does well at something and is punished when he performs poorly, he will be scared of trying anything new. This fear and anxiety are directly associated with the lack of praise. Therefore, you must praise your child.

Approval must be genuine and not over the top. You must appreciate not only any successful outcomes, but also the effort, process, and the progress your child makes. The journey towards the result is as important as the outcome itself. Therefore, don't forget to be appreciative of all that your child is. For instance, if you know that your child is learning to swim, praise him when he fearlessly jumps off the diving board. It might not seem like much to you, but it certainly is a significant step for your kid. Don't withhold the praise and be there for him.

Children are often scared of taking risks when they have low self-esteem. When you show your child that you love him and accept him the way he is and that your love is unconditional, his self-esteem will improve. Don't allow your child to believe that you will love him only when he succeeds. This kind of thinking is damaging to his overall growth. When a child feels that he is truly loved and valued, his ability to explore the various opportunities which come along his way will improve. It is quite essential to praise the process because it mostly shows your child that there are numerous ways in which something can be accomplished. You can help your child become a risk-taker by showing him that there are several right ways in which he can solve problems, puzzles, and even complete art projects.

If you want your child to be genuinely fearless while facing new challenges, then you need to show that success is not as critical as making an effort. Unless he tries, he will never know. If success is the only motivating factor, he will soon lose heart. It is quite unlikely that anyone would be good and successful at everything they try. He needs to learn to deal with failure while not giving up his willingness to try different things. Encourage him to put his best foot forward and motivate him to try as hard as he can. Whenever you notice that your child is taking a risk at trying something he usually avoided, make sure you express your appreciation. Tell him that you're proud of him, and you appreciate what he is doing. Real appreciation will certainly increase his chances of wanting to try new things in the future.

Adventure Diary

The way your child deals with a situation primarily depends on the way he views it. Instead of thinking that a challenge is intimidating, if he thinks it is exciting, then the way he deals with it will change. This change in attitude will give him the strength required to keep going and unlock his full potential. So, how do you propose to change this perspective? Well, I think the simplest thing you can do this is by maintaining an adventure diary. In this journal, make a note of all the adventures your child had because he tried something new. Read about all the different times when your child showed a lot of courage and tried something new. You must keep updating this journal regularly. Whenever possible, start adding pictures to this journal and make it look more creative and appealing. If your child is interested, then encourage him to draw all the fun moments he experienced and allow him to decorate this adventure diary the way he wants. Apart from the adventures, you must also include details about the way your child performed and the fun he had. So, the next time you notice that your child is a little apprehensive about trying something new, it's time to bring out the adventure diary and talk about all the fun experiences he's had in the past. This will give him the necessary courage to try something new.

Asking Questions

When you notice that your child is scared of trying new things or is worried about challenges, then here are a couple of questions you can ask.

- Is there something you want to do but are scared of trying? Is anything I can do to help you?
- Do you think that everyone is naturally good at whatever they do?
- How long they think it takes for a person to learn something new, like learning to swim, playing a new sport, or even an instrument?
- Are there things that some people seem to be really good at without learning or even practicing? (Your child might not have many answers to this question.)
- Is there any activity that used to seem tricky to you, but is easier now?

By asking these questions, you are essentially encouraging him to let go of his fears. You are showing him that he has the skills required to try whatever he wants. By talking about the things that no longer seem intimidating, you are encouraging him to have a little faith in his abilities.

Apart from this, here are a couple of other questions you can ask to help put your child's fears in perspective.

- Do you think that's the worst thing to happen?
- Is there any proof that what you think will happen?
- Could you do anything to change it?
- If your friend was feeling the way you are feeling, what would you tell your friend?

When you start talking to your child about trying new things, ensure that it is a conversation instead of a lecture. It needs to be an active dialogue, and must never be a monologue. Your chifocusedld will quickly get bored and lose interest if you are the only one who is talking. Instead, keep an open mind and listen to your child's worries. Even if it doesn't seem like much to you, it is an obstacle for him. Therefore, be mindful of the language you use while talking to him.

Scheduled Breaks

It is vital that you encourage your child to take risks, but you must not push too hard. His experience needs to be positive whenever he tries something new or else he will never want to try anything new in the future. If you know he has certain limitations, don't push past them. Give him a couple of breaks so that he can re-energize himself and then get back to the task at hand. Small breaks will make him feel comfortable as well as calm while trying new things. This, in turn, will help lend a positive tone to his entire experience.

If the task at hand requires your child to sit at a single spot for a long period or if it's an academic task, then start using a simple activity known as brain breaks. This technique will help him feel more focused and relaxed. It essentially relates to the incorporation of certain small activities that disrupt the monotony of the task at hand. For instance, after studying for 20 minutes, you can give your child a brain break. Maybe you can play a simple game of rock, paper scissors or play other games such as Simon Says. Apart from this, you can also sing a fun song like the hokey pokey or anything else. Brain breaks are silly and enjoyable activities that take away the severe and monotonous tone of the task. It helps to lift his spirits and refresh his mind so he can get back to work feeling more relaxed. When his overall mood has improved, then his ability to concentrate will also improve. Brain breaks also make learning fun!

Dress Rehearsals

If your child has any anxiety about dealing with social situations, then conducting dress rehearsals at home can be quite helpful. For instance, if your child gets awkward in social settings or has anxiety while talking to others, then here's a simple activity you can do. Have your entire family sit down at the dinner table so that your child can start practicing how he can meet others and start conversations with them. A dress rehearsal is a simple technique that helps familiarize your child with a new situation. Once he is familiar with the setting, he becomes more comfortable with himself, and any fear he experiences will also fade away.

Concentrate on Your Child's Needs

Apart from following all the different duties and strategies discussed in the previous section, you must concentrate on catering to a couple of your child's needs. If you want your child to become fearless and try new things enthusiastically, then there are a couple of traits you must concentrate on. You will learn about the different traits that are important to your child's overall development and how you can help this process.

Autonomy

Everyone desires autonomy. Autonomy gives you the ability to be in control of your life, take care of yourself, and make decisions for yourself. It's not just adults, but even children desire autonomy. An underlying sense of autonomy comes from the realization that your child possesses the skills required to take care of himself. It essentially refers to a sense of "I can do this." As a parent, it would be your first instinct to help your child and remove any challenges he faces in life. At the first sign of trouble, a lot of parents tend to swoop in and help their kids fix all problems. Well, if you tend to do this, then it is time you stop doing this. You are required to give your child a little autonomy in his life. At times, the best thing you can do is take a step back and allow him to take care of himself. It can be something as simple as choosing his clothes, tying his shoelaces, or even getting dressed by himself. Allow your child to draw his baths or showers, and maybe also fix some simple snacks for himself. These simple tasks might not mean a lot to you, but they give your child a feeling of being in control.

Confidence

Another important trait you must work on is developing a sense of confidence in your child. Some children are naturally self-confident, while others require a little push. As a parent, it is your duty to provide your child with all the tools he requires to become a self-confident individual. If autonomy is about an "I can do this" mindset, then confidence is about an "I CAN DO THIS" mindset. Self-confidence stems from a belief in one's skills and abilities. To improve your child's confidence, you must start celebrating all the successes he attains. Regardless of whether the success is big or small, learn to appreciate your child and celebrate these wins for him. If not you, then who else will do this for your kid? Simple sentences like, "it was difficult, but I am proud of how you managed to complete it." Something as simple as this can be a boost for your child's confidence. Make sure that you incorporate certain encouraging words into your daily conversations. Also, encourage your child to celebrate himself. Whenever he does something right, encourage him to pat himself on the back and say, "I did well." Teach him that confidence doesn't have to come from someone else and that there is plenty of it within him. All he needs to do is reach within and use his confidence.

Security

There is a lot of comfort in knowing that you're safe and secure. I'm sure even your child feels the same. The simplest way in which you can improve your child's sense of security is by spending quality time with him. Listen patiently and carefully whenever he talks. Apart from this, try to understand what he requires. Cater to his basic needs and talk to him about his emotions and feelings.

Resilience

We all require a little resilience to get through the challenge's life throws along our way. When a child is resilient, he will become capable of not just dealing with disappointment or an obstacle, but he knows that he will survive. This belief is important for his overall growth and development. Teach your child that it is okay to make mistakes and that everyone makes mistakes. Don't resort to punishing him whenever he makes a mistake. Instead, sit with him and work out how the mistake can be fixed. Teach him the skills required for problem solving and damage control. Allow him to take responsibility for his mistakes and encourage him to learn his lessons. The best way to go about doing this is by modeling good behavior. Whenever you make a mistake, acknowledge the mistake, and start making an effort to rectify the damage done.

As you start working on these basic traits your child requires, you will notice that your child is more enthusiastic to try new things. He will finally be able to step outside his comfort zone and try new activities and face challenges without getting scared. Once he is equipped with the belief that he can deal with whatever happens, he will be more inclined to try new things. Also, by helping your child develop this trait, you can effectively strengthen the bond you share. While encouraging your child, don't resort to using incentives. Your child must not try new things because he knows he will be rewarded by the end of it. You can use positive reinforcement but avoid using any materialistic gifts or rewards.

If you want your child to explore his full potential and make the most of his abilities, then he needs to try different things in life. To do this, he needs to change the way he views obstacles and challenges. This is where you come in! Once you start following these strategies, you will realize that your child is more enthusiastic and excited to face challenges in life. Apart from this, he will seem less scared and intimidated whenever he faces such situations. However, as with any other change, you are required to be consistent and regular in your efforts. You cannot use one of the strategies once in a while and expect them to work. Apart from all this, ensure that your child is communicating with you. When the lines of communication are open and clear between you two, he can talk to you about his fears. Whenever your child is talking to you about his fears are apprehensions, don't brush them off. Try to understand why he is experiencing such fear. Once you understand the reasons, it becomes easier to solve his problems.

NOTES:

_____

_____

_____

_____

_____

_____

_____

_____

_____

_____

_____

_____

_____

CHAPTER 6

Help Them Overcome the Fear of Failure

The fear of failure is quite real, and it can hold a person back from unlocking his true potential. Whenever a child is worried about failing, he usually responds to any challenges he faces by doing either of the following.

- He might give up even before he starts and thereby avoids the chance of failure.
- He might get quite upset and put himself down when he doesn't understand something on the first try. This results in anxiety related to performance.

The fear of failure is quite common, and I have noticed it in one of my kids too. When my son was five years old, he often used to get frustrated whenever he ran into any difficulties. It could be something as simple as unscrewing the lid on a jar. If he couldn't do it, he would get frustrated, and he would say something along the lines of, "I am not good at ____." Well, the good news is that there are ways in which you can help your child overcome this fear. In this section, you'll learn about specific strategies I used with my children to help them overcome the fear of failure.

Changing Your Attitude

Most of the things your child learns, at least during his initial years are all based on your behavior. Therefore, it is important that you are mindful of your behavior. I am primarily referring to your responses whenever you make a mistake, or you don't attain something. The attitude your child has towards failure is primarily based on your opinion about failure. There are two ways in which people usually deal with failure. They either think of it as a lesson to learn and improve, or they think of it as the end of the road.

Well, mistakes are part of life, and so is failure. You cannot be successful if you don't overcome shortcomings in life. Therefore, it is important that you teach your child not to worry about failure. Whenever you make a mistake, ensure that you're responding to it positively. Talk to your child about the lesson you learned from the mistake you made and the ways in which you think you can avoid making the same mistake in the future. Whenever you run into trouble, try to solve it. Keep doing this until you fix the problem. Whenever you notice that your child is struggling, you must not worry and don't allow anxiety to get a hold of you. Your child will quickly pick on this. Instead, try to stay as optimistic as you possibly can. In fact, go ahead and even encourage your child to make a couple of mistakes. After all, experience is the best teacher there is. There is one point you must keep in mind while you're allowing your child to make mistakes. Ensure that he takes full responsibility for his actions and doesn't get heartbroken because of a single mistake. Also, don't punish him whenever he makes a mistake. Instead, you must teach him about the ways in which he can fix this mistake and prevent making the same error in the future.

Effort Matters

It's not necessary that your child excels at everything he tries. There will be specific tasks at which he is not good enough. If that's the case, don't offer any pity and certainly don't try to comfort your child about his lack of abilities. Instead, encourage him to practice more and applaud the effort he makes. Start to concentrate on the effort instead of his ability. After all, he did try, and he's still trying. That certainly counts for something. I will give you a simple example of this technique in action. One of my kids used to struggle with algebra at school. I used to get worried that he is never going to get the grade required to make it out of high school. That's when I realized that I was focusing on the wrong thing. I was worried about his grades and was unable to see the effort he was making. So, I made a small change in the way I dealt with the situation. I stopped worrying about his grades and instead started encouraging him to concentrate on the subject. I started praising his efforts and helped him work harder. This, in turn, helped improve his grades, and now he's off to college. I couldn't have been any prouder of him than I was at that moment.

Showing Unconditional Love

Self-worth is directly associated with the fear of failure. You might not think this is a significant connection, but it matters a lot. Self-esteem essentially refers to what you believe about yourself and your values. The thoughts and opinions you have about your child essentially dictate the self-worth of your child. If your child starts to feel that you will not love him if he doesn't perform well, learn new skills, or do better at school, then his self-worth is bound to take a backseat. Instead of allowing your child to work on these faulty assumptions, it is time you change the way you deal with your child. As a parent, you are supposed to love your child unconditionally. Not just that, but you're also supposed to express your unconditional love for him. It is the only way in which he will gain the confidence required to take on any challenges. If he is worried that you will not love him if he fails, then he will be scared of trying anything new in life. The fear of failure, in this instance, stems from his reduced self-worth.

I'm positive that you don't expect perfection from your child. So, why don't you convey the same to your child? You must make him understand that regardless of whether he succeeds or fails in life, you will always be there by him. This will give him plenty of confidence and will directly improve his self-worth.

Worst-Case Scenario

Most of the anxiety and fear associated with failure often stems from spending a lot of time thinking about the worst-case scenario. There will always be a best case and a worst case scenario for every action you take. The more you think about the worst-case scenario, you will fear more to perform. This kind of fear can paralyze you. The same logic applies to your child, as well. If he spends all his time thinking about the worst possible outcomes, he will be riddled with anxiety.

Here's a simple exercise you can use with your child to help him get over his fear of failure. Take a sheet of paper and divide it into three columns. In the first column, make a list of all the possible worst-case scenarios he has come up with. In the second column, make a list of ways in which the possibility of these scenarios can be reduced. In the final column, help him come up with ways in which he can recover from the worst-case scenario. Once he makes a list of all these points, everything will become clearer and straightforward. He would probably realize that he was worried about nothing, and in fact, there was nothing to be afraid of.

Solution Matters

Usually, children tend to get so overwhelmed by the problems or the challenges they face that they completely forget about the solutions. There is a simple fact of life you must accept as a parent and that is failure is normal. So, don't worry if your child fails, start worrying if your child doesn't do anything after the failure. The way your child deals with his failure will set the tone for the rest of his life. If he takes a positive approach towards coping with failure, he will come out successful in life. At times, the best thing you can do as a parent is to give your child some space. Once you do this, it becomes easier for him to understand where he went wrong. Be there for your child, and help him deal with his problems. Instead of the challenge, start working on the solutions and encourage your child to think about the solutions too. Sit down with your child and start thinking about all the events which led up to the problem. Ask him about his actions and the consequences of his actions. Once you identified the problem, ask him about the ways in which he can fix the same problem from recurring.

Brainstorm solutions with your child. While doing this, you can always offer suggestions. However, don't directly giveaway the answers to your child's problem. You are encouraging him to think for himself. After all, you cannot live his life for him, and you cannot always fix his problems. By doing all this, you reduce your child's chances of feeling frustrated whenever he runs into an obstacle. A solution-oriented approach is the best problem-solving technique you can teach a child.

Also, encourage him to make a list of solutions. If one doesn't work, prompt him to try the next answer and keep going at it until he manages to fix his problem.

Success And Failure

It is quintessential that you start having conversations about success and failure with your child. According to your child's age, the kind of discussion you have with him will differ. Tell him that learning will not always be an easy process, and there will be times when he runs into obstacles. Apart from this, you must also inform him that failure is a very common aspect of life. If you're not sure how to go about having this conversation with your child, then here are a couple of ideas.

The simplest way to explain success is by using the iceberg analogy. The tip of the iceberg is usually the only visual aspect of it. However, there is plenty more of it that lies underwater, and therefore, not a lot of people can see it. Likewise, the only thing visible to you about a successful person is the tip of the iceberg. You don't see all the struggles, failures, and obstacles that they had to overcome to attain the success they have right now. Explain that failure is not necessarily a bad thing, and it can be a learning experience. For instance, if your child fails at something, then encourage him to learn from his mistakes and do things differently the second time around. Therefore, failure is a lesson, and it is a chance to do things better. Did you know that Michael Jordan did not make Varsity in high school? Even after this, he became one of the most successful and popular basketball players to date. How did this happen? Well, he did not give up, and he kept trying even in the face of failure. Use this example and explain failure and success to your child. Once you start having an open and honest discussion about success and failure, any fear that was attached to failure in your child's mind will slowly go away. Also, once he starts sharing his fears with you, it will become easier for him to manage the same.

Sit with your child and talk to him. Allow him to express himself freely and make a note of his thoughts. Instead of assuming that he might be experiencing a specific emotion, it is better to talk to him about it.

NOTES:

_____

_____

_____

_____

_____

_____

_____

_____

_____

_____

_____

_____

_____

_____

CHAPTER 7

Surround Them With Positive, Confident People

Company Matters

At times, it might seem like some people are always happy, and then there are those who still struggle to find some happiness. If you want your child to become a happy and confident adult, then there are a couple of things you must do. The first thing you must start concentrating on is the company your child keeps. The company, an individual, keeps matters a lot, not just for children, but adults as well. The way those around you think and behave often dictates the way you think and behave. The same applies to your child, as well. Here are five reasons why you must surround your child with positive and confident people.

Happiness is quite contagious. One of the simplest ways in which you can teach your child about happiness is to surround him with happy people. Surround him with those individuals who not only know how to create their own happiness but also share it lovingly and willingly.

Laughter is the best medicine there is. A great way in which your child can start connecting with others is through laughter. Laughter is often the symbol of fun times shared together. When you see the way a person reacts to a humorous situation, you feel yourself drawn into the situation, and the bond you share with the person improves. Likewise, the same will happen to your child too.

Everyone copes with challenging days and moments differently. If you notice that your child seems to be struggling with his emotions or something else, then why don't you spend some time with him? Sit down with him and talk to him about his problems. Maybe you can encourage him to draw inspiration from those around him. For instance, if he is feeling rather sad and lonely, ask him what his favorite TV character would do if he were in the same situation? You would probably have a couple of ideas. Once he knows these ideas, ask him to implement the same.

When you surround your child with happy people, his need to complain will reduce. Less complaining means more happiness for all those around; it helps strengthen your child's bond with all his family members. Apart from this, it also creates a pleasant environment in the household. Instead of wasting all his time complaining, he might even think about ways in which he can solve those problems.

Ask your child about his friends, and the company he keeps. Ask him if he would want to be like any of them or if he idolizes someone else's behavior. Ask him if he respects his friends and whether they respect him. If his answer is not yes to all these questions, then encourage him to make more friends.

Tips to Develop Confidence

The company, a child, spends his time with matters a lot when it comes to his overall personality and attitude. When he spends time with people who are more confident and positive, then he will become more confident and positive about himself. The thing about happiness is that it is quite contagious. So, encourage him to spend time with positive, happy, and confident individuals. As a parent, it is your duty to ensure that you model good behavior. Ensure that his friends add something positive to his life and don't bring him down. That said, I am not encouraging you to interfere and meddle with his life, but I am merely saying be mindful of the company he keeps. Confidence is vital for your child's happiness, success, and health. A confident child is better equipped to deal with negative emotions, challenges, frustration in life, handle responsibility, and also deal with peer pressure. What is the crucial factor when it comes to a child's confidence? The answer is you! You'll learn about simple techniques you can use to teach your child about confidence and happiness.

The first thing you must do is to make sure your child knows that your love is unconditional. I know I've mentioned this point a couple of times until now, but this is quite important. Unconditional love can help improve your child's overall personality. When your child knows that he is truly loved in spite of his flaws and shortcomings, he will become more confident. Once he becomes more confident, his ability to attain happiness in life increases, ensure that your child is fully aware of the fact that you will love and care for him regardless of what happens.

We all indulge in internal self-talk. Apart from all the conversations we have with those around us, we also tend to have an internal dialogue going on. This inner dialogue can have a positive or negative effect on one's thinking. For instance, if this internal dialogue is going well and is positive, you'll be filled with a sense of positivity. On the other hand, if your internal self-talk is negative and you keep telling yourself, "I am not good enough," or "I cannot do this," then you will be riddled with negativity. Children, as well as adults, engage in self-talk. Therefore, it is time you talk to your child about maintaining a positive attitude within his mind.

The simplest way in which you can make someone feel important is by using their name whenever you call them. So, start addressing your child by his name. It will make him feel important and valued. Whenever you say his name, ensure that you maintain eye contact as well.

If you want to make your child feel competent and responsible, it is time to delegate little tasks to him. Delegate age-appropriate particular tasks which will make him feel more like an adult. It also gives him a sense of control and autonomy. These factors play an essential role while developing his overall self-confidence. Once you delegate a task, ensure that you allow him the completed the way he wants. Don't interfere, and don't try to micromanage. If he makes any mistakes, you can always correct him later and teach him how he is supposed to improve his performance. The unique tasks you can assign your child include taking care of a younger sibling, taking care of a family pet, or even assisting you in the kitchen. Ensure that the task you give your child doesn't put him in any danger.

Playtime is quite fun. So, the next time you see your child play, why don't you join in? Once you do this, ensure that you don't interfere with whatever your child says. Allow your child to choose the game he wants to play and merely go along with it. Don't offer your opinions, and don't try to make any changes. Instead, listen to him. This simple activity will make him feel important and valued.

Regardless of whether you want to believe it or not, your child will try to copy your behavior. Perhaps this is why young children love wearing their parents' clothes or shoes. They do this because they see the parents doing it. Children will not just copy the way you behave, but they will also pick up your mindset. If you want your child to project confidence, then you need to start working on your confidence level. Once you improve your confidence, it teaches your child about self-confidence. Whenever you are in your child's presence, ensure that the language you use to describe yourself is positive and that you limit self-criticism.

Another way in which you can make your child feel like he's a valuable member of the household is by encouraging him to share his opinions and ideas. Ask him for his insight into different topics. Ensure that the topics you talk about are age-appropriate. Obviously, you cannot expect a 10-year-old to have any insightful views about world politics. Maybe the next time you go shopping for groceries, ask your child to help you come up with a list of groceries.

If you want your child to feel more confident and capable, then encourage him to set goals for himself. You will need to teach him about goals, and help him set up specific, measurable, attainable, realistic, and time-bound goals. If he sets rather lofty goals for himself, then he is merely setting himself up for failure. While setting goals, ask him why he wants to attain something and what he would do if he runs into any obstacles.

When it comes to confidence and self-worth, there are two key components, and they are acceptance and love. So, whenever you are spending quality time with your child, it shows your child that you value and love him. Ensure that you spend quality time with your child and don't allow any distractions to disturb this quality time together. It can be something as simple as going for a walk after dinner, or maybe a weekly ice cream outing after the soccer practice. It doesn't have to be anything time-consuming, and even simple activities will be quite helpful. Apart from this, engage in one-on-one conversations with your child. Ask him how his day was, talk about the different activities he is involved in, and his likes or dislikes. Try to get to know your child as much as you can. You are required to give your child undivided attention whenever you are spending quality time with him. Get rid of all distractions and concentrate only on spending time with your child. In fact, you can also make a list of activities you and your child can indulge in. Go through the previous chapters about spending quality time with children and come up with a schedule routine that fits your needs and requirements.

A common mistake a lot of parents tend to make is that a shower that children with plenty of praise. It is important to praise your child whenever he does something right. However, there is a way to go about doing this. You must not go overboard by praising him, and certainly, you must not belittle his accomplishments. There needs to be a balance in the praise you offer if you want to improve your self-esteem. Ensure that the appreciation you offer is genuine and specific. Your praise must concentrate more on the efforts your child has made, than the results he has obtained. Don't use generalized praises like keep it up, or good job. Instead, use specific words along with examples of what you appreciate about your child. For instance, if you notice that your child has cleaned his room without you asking, then you must praise him. Tell him that you are pleasantly surprised and appreciate how well he has cleaned the room.

In the previous chapters, we discussed the damaging effects of comparison. If you want your child to become more confident, then you must resist comparing him with others. If you want your child to behave better, perform well at school, or do something else, then instead of comparing, start setting specific benchmarks for him. Encourage him to do better and give him the support required to do better.

Another simple and easy way in which you can boost your child's confidence is by accidentally letting him overhear you praising his achievements. When your child realizes that you talk about her positively when he is not around, he will feel better about himself. Children, at times, are skeptical whenever they receive direct praise. So, when he accidentally hears you repeat this praise to others, he will accept the praise he's been given.

You need to work on increasing your child's sense of belonging. If your child paints or does any craftwork, then display it in the family room. If he comes up with a painting, then put it on display on the fridge. There are different ways in which you can display his accomplishments. It will create a sense of belonging. I remember when one of my daughters gave me a macaroni wall art. It is still displayed proudly on my living room walls. I will never take it down, and this is a simple way of showing her how much I love her and how much she means to me.

Encourage your child to make certain age-appropriate decisions. The way you assign special tasks and chores, you must also allow your child to make certain decisions. All these factors will help make him feel more confident and efficient. It also gives him a chance to exercise his sense of autonomy. For instance, an age-appropriate decision might probably be giving your child the freedom to choose what he wants to eat for breakfast the kind of clothes he wants to wear to school. Apart from this, you can also encourage him to order from a menu whenever you go out or even select the place where he wants to go.

You must encourage him to keep trying new things and skills in life. Even if he doesn't succeed at them, appreciate the effort he makes. Never stop encouraging him and always be his cheerleader. Keep motivating him to try different things in life. This is the only way in which he can learn.

It is important for your child to discover his interests and passions. When your child finds the things at which he excels, he will gain confidence in his abilities as well as himself. So, as a parent, it is your duty to help him explore the world around him. Keep encouraging him to try different things, and when he finds something that he likes, motivate him to cultivate skills.

I'm sure you realize the importance of confidence in life. Fear is one of the biggest enemies of confidence. By going through the different tips discussed in the previous section, I'm sure that you know about the ways in which you can help your child overcome his fear of failure. Now, it is time to start using those steps to eliminate any concern your child unnecessarily harbors in his head. Encourage your child to get on with his life and think of any obstacles he faces in life is mere setbacks instead of failure. Give him the courage to keep going.

You must encourage your child to talk about his feelings. Don't criticize his thoughts and feelings when he expresses himself. Instead, listen patiently and carefully to whatever he has to say without interruptions. Once he's done talking, you can advise him or give him suggestions. When you encourage him to express his negative as well as positive emotions, it makes it easier for him to deal with them.

A simple way in which you can encourage your child to do better in life is to start to recognize his achievements. In fact, I suggest that you create a wall of fame in your house to display his accomplishments. Maybe not your living room, you can do this in his bedroom. Showcase all his achievements, such as any art projects he successfully completed, along with any academic achievements, certificates, trophies, medals, or anything else you can think of. Place all these things on his wall of fame and keep adding to it. Once the wall is complete, your child will be filled with an immense sense of satisfaction and confidence whenever he glances upon it.

Another simple way in which you can develop your child's confidence is by displaying your love. A surprise hug and a quick peck on his cheek, and maybe a pat on his back will certainly make him feel loved and cherished. It will make him feel like he belongs and will fill them with a sense of acceptance. Start showing your love and appreciation; don't hold yourself back. This is the only way in which he will know that he is truly loved.

Confidence has a significant impact on a child's life, and it is one of the most important gifts parents can give their children. If you're unsure about where to start, then start following the different strategies discussed in this chapter.

NOTES:

_____

_____

_____

_____

_____

_____

_____

_____

_____

_____

_____

_____

_____

CHAPTER 8

Encourage Them To Express Their Feelings

Understand their Emotions

Children and adults alike tend to experience a variety of emotions. Learning to deal with emotions is an important life skill. The inability to deal with overwhelming emotions is often the reason why children tend to misbehave. By teaching your child how to express his emotions constructively, you are reducing the chances of any misbehavior. When it comes to your child, his early years of development are important. It is during this time that he usually learns about the ways of the world. This is also the time during which he starts learning about his feelings, and the ways in which he can express themselves to learning about all these things can be rather overwhelming for a child. Because of their inability to understand the complexity of the emotions they feel, they usually went to frustrations and the form of temper tantrums or even emotional outbursts. Keep in mind that your child is trying to express himself in the only way he knows. Therefore, you're supposed to teach him better ways to express. In this section, you will learn about the ways in which you can help your child understands his emotions.

The feelings a child experiences daily might seem alien to him, at least initially. Once you start naming these feelings, he will become more comfortable with them. For instance, if you notice that your child gets upset whenever you go to work, it is time to name this emotion. You can do this by saying something along the lines of, "you are sad because you have to say bye whenever mommy has to go to work." Another way in which you can teach him about emotions is while he is engaged in his daily activities. For instance, you can say something like "You are upset because playtime is over." You can also use your child's favorite TV shows and cartoon characters to teach him more about emotions. Once your child can name his feelings and emotions, you can concentrate on developing his emotional vocabulary. Teach age-appropriate feeling words to your child. As he grows older, you can start explaining more complicated feelings. For instance, the basic feelings words you can teach all 3 to 5-year old are happiness, sadness, joy, and fear. You can teach more complicated emotions like anxiety and stress to a 10 or 12-year-old.

Once you teach feeling words to him, it is time to teach him how to express his emotions. The expression of emotions is almost as important as the emotions he feels. If he fails to express them constructively, it will only cause trouble for him later in life. The best way to teach him about the expression of feeling is by modeling good behavior. Create opportunities wherein your child can come up with different solutions according to the situation. You will learn more about this in the subsequent sections.

Whenever you notice that your child is getting upset or overwhelmed, the best thing you can do is to enable your child to reconnect with you. While doing this, try to view things from a child's perspective. For instance, a baby usually calms down when he can feel his parents are around him, holding him and soothing him. Likewise, a preschooler might need to feel connected to his parents to feel better. Once you try to see something from a child's perspective, it gives you a better idea of how to handle it. In fact, the simplest thing you can do is quickly hug your child whenever you notice that he's about to have an angry outburst. There's something about a warm hug that can calm down even the angriest of children.

There are times when you will be tempted to discipline your child. Whenever you think about disciplining your child's misbehavior, avoid resorting to physical forms of punishment. Regardless of what the child does, never spank him. You must not shame your child while disciplining him. This kind of punishment often punishes the child instead of fixing his behavior. Your child might start listening to you because he's scared of the punishment he will receive. Well, this is not the right way to teach good behavior. Instead, concentrate on teaching your child about the ways in which he can manage his emotions. Instead of encouraging him to hide his feelings and bottle his emotions and allow him to express it constructively.

Whenever you notice that your child is talking about feelings, you must offer compliments and praise him for the same. By doing this, you are using a simple technique of positive reinforcement. By praising good behavior, you're encouraging his inherent inclination to replicate the same behavior in the future. Once he knows that his parents are happy with the way he is behaving, he will be more tempted to do the same in the future. Also, make sure that you tell him that you're proud of him for reaching out to you. Make a note of all the way your child expressing himself and his feeling.

A child needs to know that it is perfectly fine to express all the emotions he does. However, he must also understand that there is a way to express those emotions. Start practicing all the different techniques given in this section, and you will see a change in his behavior. It will take plenty of time, attention, consistency, and even lots of love on your part to teach him how to change. But trust me, your efforts will pay off, and the results will leave you pleasantly surprised, so start working with your child.

Express their Emotions

Now that you're aware of the ways in which you can help your child identify his emotions, it is time to teach him about the expression of the same. If you don't allow your child to express his emotions, he will start to feel that his emotions don't matter and that he doesn't deserve to express them. Once he starts thinking like this, his self-worth will reduce. There are various things that you can do as a parent to encourage self-expression. Follow the simple tips discussed here to teach your child about self-expression.

Perhaps the simplest way in which you can teach your child about expressing his emotions is by talking about your feelings. You are required to be a good role model because your child is constantly observing and noticing you. You must use words that your child can understand and tell him what you mean whenever you introduce a new feeling word. Apart from the examples discussed in the previous section, you can also start teaching him other feeling words. For instance, you can say something along the lines of, "I feel a little sad that daddy's gone away for a couple of days. I will miss him." Whenever you feel an emotion, express yourself verbally so that your child can understand. This is a great way to teach him about his emotions.

You must avoid suppressing your emotions and encourage your child to never suppress his emotions. This is quite important, never forget to teach your child this lesson. Your child must never come to the conclusion that his feelings are not important or that you don't care about what he feels. So don't use sentences like, "Don't you dare get mad at me," "If you start whining once again, no more TV for you," or "There is always something wrong with you." When you start using sentences like this, your child firmly believes that his feelings are not important and that he must not feel whatever he is feeling. This is detrimental to his emotional development. If your child starts forming a belief that he is not worthy of your love and attention, then it will certainly lead to other developmental issues. I won't be surprised if he starts to develop low self-esteem and low self-confidence because he believes that his opinions and feelings are insignificant.

There needs to be balance in everything that you do in life. Every function has a limit, and once this limit exceeds, there is no balance. This is a simple principle you must apply to all aspects of your life, and parenting is not an exception. Never go overboard, and don't overdo it. You want your child to be well adjusted and well balanced. You need to encourage him to express his feelings as honestly and clearly as he possibly can. While doing this, you must also teach him to represent them in a positive and desirable manner. Your child must not think that it is okay to express his feeling at the cost of hurting others. This is why you must draw a line and help him address his feelings constructively. For instance, if he is upset about someone else's behavior, it is not okay for him to verbally lash out at that person merely because he's expressing himself. Whenever you notice that your child is not expressing himself the way you desire, it is time to sit down and have a little chat with him.

You need to be approachable. If your child starts getting scared about the way you react to whatever he has to say, he will begin to suppress his feelings. There always needs to be an open channel of communication between a parent and the child. Ensure that you're doing everything on your end to keep this channel open and transparent. If your child starts hesitating or getting anxious about sharing his emotions, he will withdraw. You need to be approachable. Therefore, start being mindful of your body language as well as the words you use whenever you're communicating with your child. Keep your body language open and inviting. That means you must stop crossing your arms whenever you stand while talking to your child and don't stare at him aggressively. Keep in mind that your physical presence is quite dominating when compared to that of the child. Remember this whenever you are communicating with your child. In fact, I suggest that you sit down so that you and your child are at the same level and you can maintain eye contact.

You must encourage your child to start labeling his emotions. There will be times when your child experiences a painful emotion, and he starts acting out. During such moments, it is time to teach him about the emotion he's expressing. For instance, if he starts throwing a temper tantrum because he's not allowed to play with his favorite toy, then use this opportunity to teach him about anger. Once he starts labeling his emotions, it will make it easier for him to communicate the same with you. Once he expresses his emotions to you, it becomes easier to handle them. In fact, you can sit with your child and come up with a plan of action for dealing with all his emotions.

Always keep your calm whenever your child is expressing himself. Even if he's having a full-blown breakdown in public or is throwing a temper tantrum in fancy restaurants, you must keep your calm. If you start losing your calm and start shouting at your child at that time, it will not do either of you any good. In fact, it will harm the relationship you share with your child. I'm not saying that you must merely stand and watch your child misbehave, but there are better ways to control your child's behavior than yelling. Once your child is calm, it is time to have a talk about the same with him. Don't yell at him in public, don't spank him, and don't raise your voice unnecessarily. If your child is misbehaving in a restaurant, calmly take him outside for a couple of minutes and allow him to cool down. Maybe you can ask them why he's acting out. Usually, children are quite good at conveying what they require as long as the parent is willing to listen. So, become a good listener and listen to your child's troubles.

You must become an empathetic listener. Being an empathetic listener means helping someone see that you not only understand them but have also heard everything they had to say. For instance, saying sentences like, "you look a little sad to me, why don't you tell me what happened?" By doing this, you are effectively labeling the emotion your child is feeling and are also teaching him to identify his feelings. Apart from this, your child will also be happy that you are paying attention to him. A combination of these factors is quintessential for his emotional development. Once he understands that you are listening to him and will help him, he will be more open to talking about whatever problem that's bothering him.

At times, even the best of us require a little help. There is no harm or shame in asking for help. Therefore, it is time to teach your child the same. Demonstrate the way in which you ask for help so that he can start imitating your behavior in the future.

By following these simple steps, you can teach your child to manage and express his emotions adequately. Write down your experiences and any changes you might want to make in future.

NOTES:

_____

_____

_____

_____

_____

_____

_____

_____

_____

_____

_____

_____

_____

_____

CHAPTER 9

Make Sure They Know You Are Upset With Their Choices, Not With Who They Are

At times, you will undoubtedly get upset with the kind of behavior your child portrays. This is inevitable, and there is nothing you can do to escape such situations. The one thing you can do is manage your reaction in such circumstances. One fine day I came home after running errands all day long and noticed that my child had scribbled on the living room wall with my favorite lipstick. I could have lashed out at my child, but instead, I took my child and cleaned him up first. And then, I made sure that he understood I was upset with his choices and his behavior. You can be upset with your child's behavior, but never be bothered with the kind of person he is. Learn to differentiate between these two concepts. While offering criticism, you must ensure that you make it abundantly clear that it is your child's actions you're upset with and not who he is as an individual.

You need to teach your child not to do anything he doesn't want to because of guilt. When you start giving into guilty feelings, you are essentially teaching your child that guilt is a tolerable emotion. If you use guilt to make your child do anything, then he will always have a tough time saying "No" to anyone. For instance, he would readily agree even when he doesn't want to because someone said, "If you love me, you will do this for me." You need to show your child that even though you feel guilty at times, you will not allow that uncomfortable emotion to guide your decisions. You need to teach your child about right and wrong.

Children often indulge in pity parties. You must not be a part of it. For instance, your child might start victimizing himself whenever he scores poorly on a test or is benched for a season. It is but natural that your child will start feeling bad. It is okay to feel bad, but it is not okay to wallow in sadness. Don't be a part of this. Your child needs to understand that life isn't always fair, and he will face obstacles. Instead of encouraging him by showing unrequited sympathy, teach him to face obstacles and challenges.

It is okay to be concerned about your child's well-being. In fact, it is your duty as a parent to ensure that your child is always safe and protected. However, you must not allow this fear to dictate all your decisions as a parent. You need to show your child that fear is part and parcel of life. However, the way he deals with fear essentially sets a tone for the rest of his life. Teach him to handle and manage his anxiety effectively. Fear is seldom logical, and only by overcoming his fears will he be successful in life.

At times, it might seem like your child is the center of your universe. Your life should not revolve around your child's life regardless of how much you love him. You need to have your own priorities in life. If you drop everything and make your life's purpose only cater to your child's needs, he will start to develop unnecessary feelings of entitlement. In fact, he will start believing that he is entitled to all the attention in the world. If you don't want him to become a self-absorbed adult, then you need to teach him to focus on the world around him and not just himself.

Stop being a perfectionist. Stop expecting perfection from yourself as well as your kids. By doing this, you can effectively take away any unnecessary stress away from your shoulders as well as your child's. Instead, teach your child that it is okay to make mistakes, and it is okay to fail. After all, it is part and parcel of life. When a child strives to become the best version of himself, his self-worth will improve. Apart from this, he will also start behaving better.

As a parent, you must always retain control and must never allow your child to overpower you. For instance, you cannot give a toddler a choice to decide where the family can go for a vacation. However, you can allow him to pick the nightdress he would like to wear to bed. The decision-making powers you give your children must be age-appropriate. It is okay that you want to teach your child as an equal, but you must take into consideration his mental maturity. If you start giving him too much control at a young age, he will become dominating. It is important to maintain the family hierarchy while giving your child a little control.

You must not allow your child to avoid responsibilities. If you keep allowing him to skip chores or not take up his share of household responsibilities, he will never gain the mental strength required to become a responsible adult. I know you might be trying to give him a carefree childhood, but it is also your responsibility to teach him to be accountable.

Every parent would want to protect his child from sadness as well as anxiety. However, your child cannot grow in life if he doesn't experience such feelings. Only when he faces any negative emotions and overcome such emotions successfully will he be able to become a mature adult. After all, life is seldom fair. If he doesn't understand how to tolerate discomfort, he will not get ahead in life.

Keep in mind that your child is a different entity from you. Even if it feels like he is a part of you, he isn't. You need to understand that you're not responsible for the way he feels. Until a certain age, you can help your child regulate his emotions. However, after a point, your child needs to learn to control and understand his emotions himself. After all, he cannot expect his parents to fix everything for him in life.

You need to understand the difference between punishment and discipline. Punishment usually involves making a child suffer the cause of his misbehavior or wrongdoing. Discipline, on the other hand, is about teaching how to rectify his behavior. For instance, if you take away your child's TV privileges if he doesn't clean his room, you are essentially punishing him. However, if you explain why he needs to clean his room, you are disciplining your child. A disciplined child is always better than a child who fears punishment.

Never encourage your child's poor behavior. There will be times when your child starts whining for no reason or throws a tantrum for no good reason. In such instances, you might want to give in to your child's whims to calm him down. It is quite tempting; I know that. However, please refrain from doing this. If you keep giving in to your child's demands, he will conclude that by behaving poorly can get whatever he wants. This the kind of behavior you are supposed to condemn as an adult. It is your responsibility to teach him that such action is undesirable, and the consequences of such behavior will always be bad.

NOTES:

_____

_____

_____

_____

_____

_____

_____

_____

_____

_____

_____

_____

_____

CHAPTER 10

Treat Mistakes As Building Blocks For Learning

Making mistakes is quite common. After all, we are all humans, and we tend to get things wrong once in a while. It is also essential to learn from other people's mistakes. Only when you learn your lesson will you not make the same mistake in the future. An important lesson all parents need to know is about when they're required to step in and when they need to step back and merely observe. I know, it is not necessarily easy to assume the role of a silent spectator. For the sake of your child's maturity and development, you are supposed to allow things to unfold. However, they do.

There is an incident I would like to share with you. One fine day, I walk into the kitchen and notice that my bright 12-year old is trying to place a fork in a toaster! I was aghast; after all, I expected him to know better. He usually had the presence of mind to distinguish between good and dangerous behavior. In this instance, it looked like he somehow wasn't aware of the dangers of electrocution.

I know that it is heartbreakingly painful to watch your children make mistakes- this goes for any physical danger or even heartbreak- regardless of whether your child is falling off a tree or had a falling out with his friends. It would be a basic instinct to try and protect him from whatever harm that's awaiting him. All that said, the most important lessons they learn in their lives usually come from making mistakes. Once you make a mistake and then get back on track after the mistake, it gives them a tremendous sense of self-confidence to keep going. An important aspect of emotional intelligence is understanding whether you made a mistake or not. If you want your child to cope with everything that life throws his way, it is important that you understand how to control his anger as well as frustration.

Young children are seldom socially conscious. The association of a mistake with shame is formed only when the child starts to grow. Most children usually are afraid of making mistakes because they are worried about their parent's reaction. For instance, if you express anger or disappointment when your child makes a mistake, he will be afraid of disappointing you. Once he starts developing such an association in his mind, he will be associating failure with fear. If he starts fearing failure, he will never learn from his experiences. In fact, he might not even attempt new things because he's worried that he will fail. This worrying is directly associated with your response to a specific situation.

I am pretty sure that if you take a moment and think about it, you can recollect some events from your childhood where you felt a little humiliated, and these instances enabled you to link fear with failure. Think about all such experiences, which made you feel anxious and worried while growing up. Once you identify these emotions and situations, you will be better equipped to deal with what your child is experiencing. Also, you can start taking steps to ensure that you don't make the same mistakes your parents made when you were a kid. A lot of parents will readily jump in to help the child fix their mistakes. I know your intentions are well-meaning, but you're doing more harm to your child than good. Don't swoop in and save the day. Allow him to understand the consequences of his actions. The best way he can learn is by experiencing the consequences of his actions. When you start jumping to fix his mistakes, it is essentially counter-productive to good behavior.

You need to understand the effect of positive and negative feedback on your child's brain. When your child is quite young, especially under the age of 12, his brain is quite good at understanding positive feedback. However, the part of his brain, which usually processes negative feedback, is underdeveloped before the age of 12. So, even if you provide negative feedback, the chances of your little one processing it is quite slim. There are only two circumstances wherein you're supposed to help your child whenever he makes a mistake. The first situation is when he is in any physical danger, and the second one is when any consequences for bad behavior will not be apparent for a while.

An example of this would be when you notice that your child is lying to his friend, but the consequence of this lie will not come to light until the following week. If you notice that your child is doing something worrisome, but you are unable to see an instant percussion for the same, then you are supposed to create one. In the previous example, you notice that your child is lying. So, what will you do? Well, for starters, you can casually expose the lie. Keep in mind that you are not supposed to shame him while doing this. Once you shame him, he will form a negative association between mistakes and failure.

I want you to take a moment and answer this question honestly. What is your job as a parent? If your answer is always to protect the child, then your style of parenting is often based on fear. Whenever your decisions as a parent stem from the fact that you're trying to avoid something, it tends to create anxiety for your child. Apart from this, it can also lead to overprotectiveness and hyper-vigilance on a parent's part. If that's the case, then you will be constantly tempted to keep reminding your child what he is supposed to do. Even if your child is quite competent and capable, if you constantly keep giving him instructions, he will start believing that he cannot do anything until he receives instructions from someone else.

If your answer to the previous question is, "I want to raise a child who can thrive in any situation," then your parenting style gives you the freedom to believe that your child can learn from his mistakes. A lot of parents fail to understand that children are quite resilient. We seem to think that they are rather delicate because of that physical stature. However, they are good at grasping the gravity of the situation the way adults do.

Do you think your child is a miniature version of yourself or if he has a unique individuality? Regardless of all the qualities and traits that are inherited from you and your partner, it is not necessary that he makes the same mistakes you did. One of the best gifts you can bestow upon your child is the gift of Independence. Allow him to make his own decisions. Most parents tend to act as managers instead of parents. I think that it is a great idea to start delegating responsibilities to your child. Ensure that the responsibilities are age-appropriate.

Whenever you give any responsibility to your child, give him the power to make his own decisions and allow him to face the consequences of his actions as well. The way your child perceives things will always be different from the way you view it. What might seem wrong to you might seem right to your child. So, before you decide that your child has made a mistake, try to see it from his perspective. It will give you a better understanding of the way he thinks, and you will be in a better position to deal with the situation as well. Once you start allowing your child to make mistakes, you help strengthen his resolve. Apart from this, it also gives him the assurance that he can handle whatever comes in life and he will become more confident. Mistakes are the building blocks for success. Teach your child to deal with his mistakes instead of worrying about the mistakes he makes.

Tips To Deal With Mistakes

In this section, you will learn about simple tips you can use to deal with your child's mistakes.

Whenever your child sees you tackle all challenges with positivity and preparation, you're setting a good example for him. You need not put up a facade of perfection, but try to do your best in every situation.

Don't get frustrated whenever your child makes a mistake. Try to limit any possible damage in such situation, and stay calm. If you get upset and start yelling at him, he will be worried about making mistakes. This kind of thinking will put additional stress on his developing mind. It might also prevent him from ever trying anything else. Also, don't fix everything for him. Teach him problem solving skills and let him use them in his life.

Help your child understand that everyone makes mistakes. Encourage him to learn from his mistakes instead of dwelling on them. The only way he will become more confident is when he understands how to tackle any obstacle.

Encourage your child to try new activities. He will want to concentrate on those activities he excels at, but it is your responsibility to introduce him to new skills. Learning new skills will make your child feel quite capable and confident to tackle everything that life throws his way.

Trial and error is a great way to learn. Repress your desire to try and protect your child from failure. Your child needs to learn to deal with failure. He needs to understand that if he doesn't accomplish something, it is not the end of the road. Instead of making him fear failure, encourage him to deal with it.

Perseverance is an important life skill. You child might probably give up at the first sign of frustration or quit right after a setback. Being resilient is as important as being successful. After all, success does come from resilience.

Start encouraging your child to find his own interest. It helps develop his sense of identity while making him more confident. When he sees that he is talented at something, it will improve his self-esteem.

Learn to let go of your idea of perfection. It is time to embrace imperfection, after all life is seldom perfect. As a grown-up, you might realize this, but your little one still doesn't. Therefore, it is important to teach your child that perfection isn't always possible. Tell him that it is okay to be less than perfect, and that it makes him a human being.

A child tends to stumble and fall while he is learning to walk. He doesn't stop once he falls, instead, he tries harder the next time. Children are not afraid of making mistakes, it is only societal pressure and conditioning which makes them fear failure. It is your duty to teach him that mistakes are building blocks for learning.

Sit down with your child and calmly talk to him about his poor choices. Tell him that you are not angry and that you are merely looking out for him. You want him to be safe and that's probably the reason why you got upset.

Children tend to act out because of different reasons ranging from their inability to deal with powerful emotions to any physical discomfort. Try to understand what triggered your child to act out. Once you identify the trigger, it becomes easier to prevent any undesirable behavior in the future.

The way you view success will be quite different from the way your child perceives success. Therefore, you must be careful to not impose your values upon him. Allow him to define success for himself. To do this, he needs the freedom to explore the world around him. He might make mistakes along the way, but don't punish him for them. Teach him to avoid making the same mistakes again and encourage him to perform to the best of his abilities.

Whenever your child makes a mistake, make a note of it in your journal. If you are aware of the instances which led to the mistake, write about it along with your response to the situation. By doing this, you can analyze why your child makes those mistakes.

The style of parenting you opt for must cater to your specific situation. Stop wishing that your child was like someone else. Do you remember the saying, "the grass is always greener on the other side?" Well, this is applicable to all aspects of your life, and parenting is never an exception. Try to do the best you can for your child and encourage him to put his best foot forward. Teach him to be a better human being and stop worrying about other things.

NOTES:

_____

_____

_____

_____

_____

_____

_____

_____

_____

_____

_____

_____

_____

_____

CHAPTER 11

Don't Allow Them To Escape Reality By Spending All Their Time On The Internet Or Playing Video Games

We all live in a world that's dominated by technology. All the technological advancements we've made have certainly made our lives easier. On the downside, these changes have also brought along with them a whole new range of addictions. Addictions no longer mean substance abuse or alcoholism, but there are new forms of addictions coming up. Being addicted to virtual reality or playing video games has also been categorized as a disorder. The World Health Organization has coined the term gaming disorder to describe a compulsive need to play video games. All those children who spend most of their time gaming instead of engaging in any other activities in their life suffer from a gaming disorder. It is okay to allow your child to play video games and spend time on the internet. However, how much is too much? This is one question you must answer. Once you have an answer, it is time to enforce the same.

The side effects of gaming addiction or Internet addiction include obsessive behavior, lack of sleep, physical ailments, social isolation, and lack of physical exercise. If your child has a gaming disorder, then you might notice that he starts escaping the problems life throws his way instead of confronting them. Children who usually lead stressful lives find relief when they escape into the world of virtual reality. If your child keeps doing this, he can never become a fully functioning member of society. He might also experience symptoms of withdrawal whenever he's not allowed to spend any time playing video games or use the internet. Apart from this, he might also start being deceitful and shows no interest in other activities. Well, all these side effects are quite bad. The good news is that this problem can be easily fixed. You will learn about certain simple tips you can follow to ensure that your child doesn't stay transfixed in the world of virtual reality.

If you want to break your child's gaming disorder, then you must spend some time and talk to him about what he is doing. Tell him that it is okay to use video games as a means of entertainment, but that is not all that his life is about. Ensure that he is aware that any success he obtained in the gaming world is all virtual and will not translate to his real-life achievements. Tell him that by spending all his time in the fantasy world, he's missing out on the life that happens around them.

As a parent, you must regulate the time he spends on the internet or plays video games. For instance, ensure that he doesn't spend more than 30 to 60 minutes on a school day and not more than two hours during the weekends. You're free to decide this limit and ensure that once you set a limit, you enforce it. If you don't enforce this limit, your child will not care for the rules you make.

Always set a timer when you allow your child to play video games. I know, it sounds a little rudimentary, but this is the most effective way to ensure that he listens to your rules. Set the timer for an hour, and once the timer goes off, it signals the end of game time. Don't exceed his time limit.

Apart from this, you can also use automated blocking software to program the game to shut down once a specific time limit has reached.

If you notice that your child breaks any gaming rules you set, you must enforce consequences. If you don't enforce consequences, your child will take your word for granted. Ensure that if he breaks a rule, he cannot play video games for a while. If you start giving him any leniency and cutting slack whenever you notice that he feels a little low, he will not take you seriously.

Start encouraging your child to engage in other activities instead of just playing video games. Encourage him to go out with his friends, spend time outdoors, or even engage in any of his hobbies. Spend some time, and make a list of all his favorite hobbies and start encouraging him to participate actively. If you know that your child likes to read, then buy him his favorite books. Start engaging in conversations with him, which are not associated with the world of gaming and the internet. Find a hobby that you and your child can participate in together. Go for walks in the evening, spend some time playing catch in the park, or maybe just sit at home and have a nice discussion with each other. Maybe you both can watch a movie together. There are plenty of activities you can do together, and start making a list of the same.

If you notice that your child has a genuine problem that you're not able to fix by following the different steps discussed in this section, then it is time to seek some professional help. Don't hesitate to seek the help of a child psychologist. The sooner you fix this problem, the better it is for your child's overall development.

NOTES:

_____

_____

_____

_____

_____

_____

_____

_____

_____

_____

_____

_____

_____

CHAPTER 12

Over-Praising Kids Does More Harm Than Good

I know one of the most common solutions included in this book is related to praising your child. However, you must be mindful of the praise you give your child. Praising your child too little or too much is detrimental to his overall growth and development. When you appreciate your child's effort, it gives him the motivation to do better in life. Apart from this, it also encourages him to change his attitude towards any challenges he faces. Genuine praise helps increase his autonomy and competence while giving him the strength required to deal with his fears.

A common mistake a lot of parents make is that in their bid to help improve their child's self-esteem, they indulge in overpraising. We live in a world that's incredibly competitive, and there is no scope for mediocrity in it. Most of us spend a lot of our time focusing on a child's greatness, to define who he is as an individual that we tend to make exaggerated statements about his abilities and skills. Most often, these statements fail to reflect the child's true abilities. It is good that you want to praise your child and that you are your child's cheerleader, but you must know where to draw the line. You probably think that by telling your child, "You are incredible," "You are invincible," "You are the best," "or "You are incredible," you are being helpful. When you keep telling your child these statements repeatedly, your child will come to believe them. However, what will happen when your child realizes that he is none of the above? His self-confidence will take a massive beating, and his self-esteem will be crippled. If he doesn't get things right later, he might also feel like he has let you down. A combination of all these factors will wreak havoc on your child's emotional well-being.

Improving your child's self-esteem is not about telling your child that he is the epitome of perfection. You don't have to tell your child that he will always succeed or that he is a superstar, regardless of what he does. You might think that you are helping your child, but you're doing more harm than good. Real self-worth and self-esteem are based on the skills he has acquired and the actual accomplishments he has achieved. A lot of parents tend to build up a false sense of self by making exaggerated statements. For instance, if your child makes a painting which isn't truly good and you know it, how would you react to it? A balanced approach of parenting would be saying something like, "that is quite creative. I know how hard you worked on it."

On the other hand, overpraising would be saying something like, "Wow! That is a brilliant painting, and I think you're the next Picasso!" Now, let us assume that your child goes ahead and shows the same painting to someone else, expecting the kind of praise from them that he received from you. When other people don't react or respond favorably, your child will be confused. He will either think that others are lying to him or you are lying to him. Neither of these conclusions is desirable. A lot of parents tend to do this innocently because they are trying to make their children feel better about themselves. I think most parents do this because, on a subconscious level, they're trying to compensate for the lack of praise during their own childhood. Some parents tend to do this because they are trying to boost their own fragile ego based on their child's abilities. Instead of acknowledging the fact that the child is a mediocre artist, they would inflate their parenting ego by making exaggerated statements about their child's perceived talents.

So, the next time you start praising your child for something he did, ask yourself a simple question. Does he surely deserve to be praised? You can always appreciate the effort, but stop glorifying something which you know is not worthy of the praise you are showering him with. That said, I'm not suggesting that you must put your child down or discourage him. Always encourage his efforts. Don't start to unnecessarily fuel your child's ego because you're worried about your fragile ego. Don't try to vicariously live off your child's experiences and don't think of your child's accomplishments as a reflection of your parenting skills. Once you stop doing all this, you will realize the damaging effects of overpraising.

Inadequacy

When you create a false buildup of your child's greatness, your child will start believing that he needs to be great if he wants your love. If you indulge in overpraising, your child will also quickly catch on. He will start to feel empty on the inside because he knows that the praise he has received is unrealistic. It will make your child feel uncertain about his actual abilities. Apart from this, he might also start feeling insecure and will stop trying altogether.

Entitlement

Whenever you are overpraising your child, you are mostly doing the following to him. You are creating a feeling of entitlement in him. By overindulging and overpraising your child, you are giving him a sense that he is special and unique. It is okay to tell your child that he is unique, but it is also essential that you teach him the realities of life. If he carries a sense of entitlement into adulthood, then he will expect that life will be easier for him because you have told him he is special. When life isn't all peachy like he imagined, he will be in for a nasty disappointment. When he's unprepared for all the challenges that life throws at him, he will be caught unawares. Therefore, stop overindulging your child. Praise him when he deserves it and refrain from overpraising. This kind of over parenting that a lot of people have been indulging in is the reason why narcissism has become a dominant trait these days. A lot of young people are expecting brilliant results without any hard work. This kind of mentality will hurt your child, and he will never develop the skills required to become successful in life.

Disappointments

Parents readily make sacrifices because they want the best for their children. At times, they will go to certain extremes that their life primarily revolves around the needs of their children. When you start catering to every demand of your child regardless of how insignificant or severe it is, you are making him feel important even when he doesn't deserve it. Stop treating your child like royalty. If you keep doing this, apart from the sense of entitlement, he will also start harboring unrealistic expectations of what life is supposed to be like. He will be in for a rude disappointment when he sees that life is nothing like he imagined. As a parent, it is your responsibility to prepare your child for the realities of the world. You don't have to shield him from the harsh realities of life, instead, you must prepare him to deal with it. Stop being over-involved in your child's life. Give him help when he needs it and at other times, take a step back. You need to allow your child to live his life and allow things to unfold the way they are supposed to. When you start doing everything for him and don't let him take responsibility, he will never learn. You might think that you are helping your child, but you are essentially handicapping him for the rest of his life. He will become so dependent on you that he will be rendered incapable of doing anything for himself.

Lack Of Interest

When you start getting a little too involved in your child's accomplishments, you start over identifying yourself with your child or start investing in his greatness. By doing this, you essentially intrude in his life, and this will hurt his interest. This is especially true when you start viewing his accomplishments and achievements as a reflection of your parenting. Let me give you a simple example to help make this concept clear. There was once a young girl who loved ballet. She took pride in going to ballet lessons and performing until the day her mother became involved. Ballet had been a source of independence and confidence for the little girl, but pretty soon, her mother's presence at all the practice sessions and the unnecessary feedback from her during her dance rehearsals soon made her feel resentful and even embarrassed. She started to view ballet as a chore instead of an enjoyable activity. After a while, she lost interest in dancing altogether!

So, what can you do instead of overpraising your child while helping to develop his self-esteem? Well, you don't have to stop complimenting him or supporting him and his interests. You must start taking notice of something your child loves and offer unconditional support and encouragement in a manner that's realistic and appropriate. While doing this, avoid placing any labels. When you start labeling, you are essentially catering to your wishes and fantasies instead of your child's reality. Here are a couple of simple points you must remind yourself whenever you get an urge to overpraise your child.

- Give your child the freedom to do what he likes, and he will soon be good at it.
- Don't associate yourself with your child's success.
- Don't give him unnecessary compliments and only compliment his effort.
- Never forget to praise the effort and hard work he puts in.
- If you want your child to have an improved sense of self-worth, then you are required to give him some independence and autonomy.
- This self-worth, when it improves, will give him the required self-esteem to lead a happier and more successful life.

- When you give genuine compliments or sincerely compliment your child skills, you increase his feeling of self-worth.

NOTES:

_____

_____

_____

_____

_____

_____

_____

_____

_____

_____

_____

_____

_____

CONCLUSION

There will be times in every parent's life when they wished that their children came along with an instruction manual. Well, it would certainly make things easier, wouldn't it? However, all that's just wishful thinking. Every child is different, and so is every parent. The way someone deals with their child might not necessarily be a good fit for you. That's alright, but there are certain tips which are universally acceptable to all parents. As a mother of four kids, I have realized that even though my kids are all different from one another, specific parenting techniques work. All the information included in this book is based on my personal experience. I have tried each and every technique, and I know when they are used correctly, there are quite effective. Learning to deal with your child and teaching him the skills required to excel in life is your responsibility. You cannot avoid this responsibility, and you certainly cannot shrug it off.

Before improving your child's self-confidence, you must concentrate on yourself. Unless you seem confident, your child will not listen to you. Keep in mind that you are your child's first role model, and the kind of behavior you exhibit will have a lasting impact on his psyche. Avoid self-criticism and start modeling confidence whenever you are around your child.

You must start spending quality time with your child. Whenever you are doing this, ensure that you get rid of all distractions and that all your attention is directed towards your child. By providing quality attention, you're not only strengthening the bond you share with your child but are also fundamentally improving his self-esteem. When he feels like a valued and loved member of the household, he will become more confident.

Regardless of how well someone else's child behaves, resist the urge to compare. You might wish that your child would behave differently or that he would behave like someone else. However, this kind of thinking will do you no good. In fact, it will only put a strain on the relationship you share with the child. Apart from this, it will also put unnecessary stress on him. By comparing your child with others, you are increasing the scope for self-doubt and negativity. A child doesn't need all this. Instead, create a loving and nurturing environment for him, and he will blossom.

As a parent, you obviously love your child unconditionally, but does your child know this? If you have even an inkling of doubt that your child doesn't know this, it is time you show him. Start expressing your love to your child. This is the only way in which he will know that he is loved. Love your child, regardless of what happens, and it will give him the confidence to tackle life's challenges head-on.

You must start encouraging your child to try new things. Give him the strength required to overcome the fear of failure. Unless he tries new things, he will never be able to discover his strengths. Start being supportive of his efforts instead of concentrating on the end results. Applaud all the hard work he does and praise him for the effort he puts in. Stop worrying about the results and stop stressing your child out about the same. Once you do this, his overall performance will improve.

Start surrounding your child with those who lift his spirits and serve the ones who bring him down. Pay attention to the company he keeps and ensure that he is surrounded by positive and confident people.

Teach your child about his feelings, help him label these feelings, and encourage him to express whatever he feels. By doing this, he will be in better control to regulate his emotions and control them. Only when he does this, he will be able to exhibit good behavior.

Encourage your child to make mistakes and teach him how to deal with his mistakes. Teach him about responsibility and accepting one's faults. Encourage him to think that every mistake is a chance for learning and ensure that he learns his lesson. Make sure that your child knows that you will never be upset with who he is, but can be upset with the choices he makes. Be mindful of the language you use whenever you're talking to your child. Not just your language, but your body language too. Praise your child, but don't go overboard.

In this book, you were provided all the information you require to improve your child's level of confidence. Once your child is confident, his self-esteem will improve, and he will have the courage needed to tackle all the challenges he faces in life. Apart from this, he will also have the skills required to attempt new things and attains his goals. Therefore, by improving your child's self-confidence, you are essentially paving the way for happiness and success.

Well, I'm pretty confident that after going through this book, you have realized that there are certain areas on your parenting where you excel and areas where you lag. Once you are aware of areas where there is scope for improvement, you must follow through and improve yourself. The key to improving your child's confidence lies in your hands. It is quite easy and doable, provided you are willing to commit yourself to this process. I have delivered the solution I promised at the beginning of this book.

Now, all that's left for you to do is start implementing the different practical suggestions and strategies given in this book. While doing this, there is one thing you must keep in mind. Ensure that you are loving, caring, patient, and consistent in your efforts. You must love your child unconditionally; give him all the support he requires, and help develop his confidence. Once you do this, you will notice that your child is happy and can get what he wants from life.

Thank you and all the best!

NOTES:

_____

_____

_____

_____

_____

_____

_____

_____

_____

_____

_____

_____

LEAVE A REVIEW

Reviews mean a lot to independent authors like me who don't really have massive marketing budgets. I would like to ask one small favor of you. If you enjoyed reading this book, could you take a minute or two to leave a review? I would really love to read your honest feedback.

REFERENCES

5 Ways to Help Children Identify and Express their Emotions. (2017). Retrieved from https://www.mindchamps.org/blog/help-children-identify-express-emotions/

10 Ways to Show Your Kids You Love Them | All Pro Dad. (2019). Retrieved from https://www.allprodad.com/10-ways-to-show-your-kids-you-love-them/

10 Ways to Show Your Kids You Love Them | All Pro Dad. (2019). Retrieved from https://www.allprodad.com/10-ways-to-show-your-kids-you-love-them/

Bhandarkar, S. 101 Easy Ways to Show Your Kids Just How Absolutely Loved They Are - A Fine Parent. Retrieved from https://afineparent.com/positive-parenting-faq/101-simple-ways-to-love-your-child.html

Grose, M. (2017). Confidence-building strategies every parent should know - Parenting Ideas. Retrieved from https://www.parentingideas.com.au/blog/confidence-building-strategies-every-parent-should-know/

Here is Why You Should Never Compare Your Child to Others. (2019). Retrieved from https://www.myparentingjournal.com/should-parents-comparing-children/

How to Treat your Child's Video Game Addiction - Raise Smart Kid. (2018). Retrieved from https://www.raisesmartkid.com/10-to-16-years-old/6-articles/treat-childs-video-game-addiction

Kim, M. (2015). The Good and the Bad of Escaping to Virtual Reality. Retrieved from https://www.theatlantic.com/health/archive/2015/02/the-good-and-the-bad-of-escaping-to-virtual-reality/385134/

Morin, A. Mentally strong kids have parents who refuse to do these 13 things. Retrieved from https://www.mother.ly/child/mentally-strong-kids-have-parents-who-refuse-to-do-these-13-things

Neish, S. (2011). Let your child make mistakes. Retrieved from https://www.psychologies.co.uk/let-your-child-make-mistakes

Norman, R. (2019). A Surefire Phrase to Ease Your Child's Fear of Failure. Retrieved from https://amotherfarfromhome.com/how-to-erase-your-childs-fear-of-messing-up/

Stop Comparing Your Child with Others. (2019). Retrieved from https://www.beingtheparent.com/stop-comparing-your-child/

Taylor, J. (2009). Parenting: Fear of Failure: A Childhood Epidemic. Retrieved from https://www.psychologytoday.com/us/blog/the-power-prime/200909/parenting-fear-failure-childhood-epidemic

Taylor, J. (2019). 5 reasons to surround yourself with happy people - Happier. Retrieved from https://www.happier.com/blog/how-to-be-happier-5-reasons-to-surround-yourself-with-happy-people/

Vinopal, L. (2018). 5 Ways to Pay More Attention to Your Kid in the Same Amount of Time. Retrieved from https://www.fatherly.com/health-science/give-kids-more-attention-equal-amount-time/

Made in the USA
Middletown, DE
28 November 2020

25506966R00106